Gwathmey Siegel

Edited by Brad Collins and Diane Kasprowicz

Buildings and Projects
1982–1992

Introduction by Peter Eisenman

In loving memory of Courtney Steel

First published in the United States of America in 1993
by Rizzoli International Publications, Inc.
300 Park Avenue South, New York, New York 10010

Library of Congress Cataloging-in-Publication Data
Gwathmey Siegel : buildings and projects, 1982–1992 /
edited by Brad Collins and Diane Kasprowicz;
introduction by Peter Eisenman.
p.   cm.
ISBN 0-8478-1675-3. — ISBN 0-8478-1676-1 (pbk.)
1. Gwathmey Siegel & Associates Architects.
2. Architectural practice, International.
3. Architecture, Postmodern—United States.
I. Collins, Brad. II. Kasprowicz, Diane.
NA737.G948G83 1993   93-10438
720'.92'2—dc20   CIP

front cover: Werner Otto Hall, photo by Paul Warchol; Stadtportalhäuser, plan
back cover: Opel Residence, photo by Richard Bryant / Arcaid

Design and type composition by *Group* C INC / New Haven (BC, RF, DK, FS)

Printed and bound in Singapore

Reprinted in 1997, 2004

Contents

Peter Eisenman

In *Gravity's Rainbow,* Thomas Pynchon uses the V-2 rocket to trace the contours of an emergent world that seeks to free itself from the gravity-bound confines of the earth. It is a world that displaces the priority of ground to figure, launch to launched, and that decenters geocentric perspective altogether. Earth and V-2 become rockets, figures that no longer correspond to any previous idea of figure-ground, which instead trace new trajectories, while the earth itself is seen only as the reversed orbital projection of the rocket. Within this new world, what Pynchon describes as the inexplicable and idiosyncratic return of the V-2 to its launch site can be characterized as neither predictable nor unpredictable. Instead, it is this reversed trajectory or "turning back on itself"—a characteristic, as Pynchon notes, unique to the V-2—that defines a new kind of predictability in an unpredictability, a new kind of order based on disorder. Indeed, the retro-trajectory of the V-2 delimits a new space-and-time typology, a vectorial space and time. Its orbital apogee, that moment of turning back, defines a new temporal singularity that, within this new typology, displaces all forms of identity and essence.

This turning-back trajectory of Pynchon's V-2 rocket can also be used to describe the period of American architecture from 1968 to 1993. Specifically, this new vectorial space-and-time typology provides a useful way to characterize what can only be said to be the dissonant spatial typologies of architects Charles Gwathmey and Robert Siegel, whose orbit, while coinciding with the beginning and end points of this time of American architecture, has attempted a different trajectory.

In his analysis of contemporary architecture, Kurt Forster also uses a rocket analogy to describe the state of American architecture. But in Forster's account it is the rocket assembly, the gantry crane and the scaffolding, that has taken off, leaving the rocket steaming and sputtering on the launch pad. Forster's image of an earth-bound rocket, unwilling to move, illustrates the effects of a hyper-mobile media serving as the launchpad for an unmoving architecture. The rocket analogy thus illustrates the media's transformation of architecture into thousands of self-similar images, each only as good or as bad as the next, and each unique only by virtue of its publication. The moment these images repeat themselves they are used up. Each time a new trajectory must be projected, even though the ostensibly elusive target seems not to have moved.

It is perhaps strange and even ironic to compare American architecture from 1968 to that of 1993 in order to illustrate the idea of a "turning back upon itself." But these two dates correspond to two crucial points in the trajectory of Gwathmey Siegel's work: to their first houses and to their latest rethinking, found here in the publication of their collected work. The point of departure for this present essay is the suggestion that today these two points share a nostalgia for a lost vision and a curious kind of complexity that derives as much from the history of Europe as it does from the opportunism of America. The beginning and end points of this twenty-five-year trajectory, 1968 and 1993, present, in different guises, a similar condition of American architecture: the populist themes of a social relevance of 1968 versus the formless idea of an intellectual banality of 1993. Oddly enough, both of these positions argue against what they perceive to be high art and architecture in any form, against both Howard Roark and the star system created by the media. Both of these anti-architectural positions frame the critical position of the work of Gwathmey Siegel,* and both stand against any kind of formalism, or theory of formalism, understood to be hostile to social program and the texture of built materiality. Each of these positions denies the possibility of an inherent nature of architecture as necessarily formal (as opposed to aesthetic or any other essentialism) and is thus fearful of the ideological energy inherent in such a formulation. This is because theories of architecture were usually formulated as categorical treatises. These treatises concerned themselves with issues of aesthetics, function, and meaning. Formalism attempts to move from form as the idea of category—i.e., of static types—to discussions of a dynamic forming, such as the idea of a vectorial space and time.

To understand the nature of such a critical framing of the Gwathmey Siegel work within what is best described as a kind of pragmatic formalism, it is important to go back to the beginnings of Gwathmey Siegel, to *Five Architects* and their evolution from the CASE group, which dates from 1964 to 1972. Present at the first CASE meeting were Colin Rowe and Vincent Scully: Rowe was a protagonist of a European modernism that can be traced from Palladio to Le Corbusier;

* When I speak of the work of Gwathmey Siegel, it will be seen that I am speaking of their houses. It is interesting, in this context, that they refer to their houses as residences, which for me wrongly situates their formal value in the realm of semantics.

Shore Birds, or the Rocket's Red Glare

Scully was a protagonist of an American fundamentalism that can be traced from Jefferson to Wright. With Scully and Venturi's precipitous departure from that first meeting—their ostensible reason being that they were interested in building, not in theorizing—a critical split in American architecture occurred. Indeed it was this theme of building versus theory commingled with notions of social relevance that in the late 1960s made the appearance of Gwathmey Siegel's houses, first as objects themselves and then in their inclusion in *Five Architects*, all the more polemical. If we are to believe Kenneth Frampton, the work of Gwathmey Siegel is an amalgam of Rowe and Scully—Le Corbusier by day and Wright by night, as Colin Rowe is fond of saying; shingle style in modernist drag. Comfortable neither with the theorizing of Rowe nor with the homilies of Scully, the work of Gwathmey Siegel has always seemed out of place in *Five Architects*. This is because their work derives from neither source. That is to say, any stylistic reading of Le Corbusier that may have found its way into their forms is neither ideological nor nostalgic for a new utopia. The same must be said for the reading of their work as an example of an American stick style, as the expression of individual ruggedness—an attitude which, in any case, quickly disappears after the first few houses. These readings miss the unique critical and formal content of their work, which places it outside of the discourse of *Five Architects*.

Five Architects was a stylistic, not a critical, context. To read the work of Gwathmey Siegel as a variation on the sophisticated collages of Richard Meier or Michael Graves, collages which at that time reinscribed a reading of European modernism into contemporary American thought, diffuses the possible reading of a critical formal content of their work. Rather, it is more appropriate to locate their work between the above-mentioned split in American architecture. For it is in this seam, between gratuitous imagery on the one hand and pandering historicism on the other, that their work becomes of critical interest. It is only when one discards the literal programmatic readings and metaphoric analogies, when the "isms" of architecture have been exhausted, that another possible interpretation emerges—that of a mute, unforgiving formalism.

In the end, it can be argued that all architecture of substance must come to rest in the bedrock of such a discourse. And it is only there that one can locate the critical content of the Gwathmey Siegel projects. But if this is the case, if formalism can be of critical value, then why does the mere mention of formalism create such hostility when compared to any other ism? Why is it that formalism is always a pejorative description of architecture that seems to deny social program and site? Can this only be explained as uninformed prejudice? Perhaps not. At first reading, wrongly or rightly the term suggests only a narrowly defined understanding of formalism as a doctrinaire approach that supposedly privileges aesthetic form to the exclusion of function and content. Even the words trans*form*ation and *form*alization, which begin to speak of process, do not carry the edge that formalism does. But formalism can have many different incarnations, which, rather than excluding program, meaning, and even process, issue from them.

To cite formalism as a condition of the Gwathmey Siegel work one must first understand what would constitute such an American or pragmatic formalism. As it has been traditionally understood, American architecture was forged on the anvil of pragmatism and nurtured in the soil of a primitive naturalism. This understanding helped to produce an environment hostile to theory (as opposed to history) and particularly to any idea of a formal theory. Theory was thought to be an abstract, elitist idea, and thus thought to inhibit the natural right of individual expression. However, from Jefferson's gridding of America, which was the ultimate pragmatic and totalizing gesture in all of Western planning, to Wright's Prairie houses, the concept of a fundamental individualism was always thought to be the foundation for American architecture. This was as much true in 1968 when America's supposed answer to modernism, Louis Kahn, held sway, as it was twenty-five years earlier in 1943, when modernism was dying on the battlefields of Europe.

By 1943 the influence of European modernism—the architectural manifestation of a political ideology founded on an idea of the good society—had been neutralized politically if not aesthetically in American architecture. The symbols of the good life proffered by European modernism were transformed into the images of American corporate identity and the American suburban house. In 1968 the architectural battlefield saw the return of a theoretical and formal consciousness originally spawned in European modernism, which was opposed to an American vernacular seen as a neo-Romantic concern about the form of the single-family house. For the latter, European modernism was too cold, too austere, too collective, and too theoretical; for the former, American individualism was too sentimental, too pragmatic, too anti-intellectual, and, most of all, had nothing to do with the spirit of the age. What is interesting is that the formalism of Gwathmey Siegel has little to do with either ideology. Rather, it is located in what can be called a pragmatic formalism. Pragmatic formalism is defined when the conceptual mechanisms that inform what can be called in this particular case a formal ordering—i.e., hollowing, rotation, extension, etc.—at the same time inform the vectoring of movement in the building. Thus, in the early houses the hollowing mechanism is often figured as a spiral stair, while in later houses the extending mechanism is also the ramped circulation element. In both cases the results of the process are not static but dynamic, and thus the experience of the human body in motion conforms to the formal organization; the body and the mind understand space simultaneously. This type of conceptualization has little to do with function, program, or meaning qua house, rather it has to do with the mechanics of a body in space and a dynamic form. Thus the formalisms reside ultimately in those integers of circulation, the interstitial or contingent spaces, that now figure the organization.

It is precisely this different view of what constitutes a formal spatial organization that differentiates Gwathmey Siegel's work from other more recent formalisms such as neo-high-tech and retro-neoclassicism, each of which in its own way attempts to produce the objective gloss that ostensibly characterizes all formalism. It is important to note that Gwathmey Siegel's formalism, in the ways the term will be used here, refers to the adherence to an internal consistency that derives from its own logic—an intra- as opposed to an inter-textuality. The studious avoidance of these latter-day high jinks allows Gwathmey Siegel to maintain a mute silence with respect not only to their closest contemporaries but also with respect to their own work. Some have argued, in fact, that this silence epitomizes an almost dumb obstinacy in the face of the need for change. And yet it is precisely this stubbornness and its unchanging quality that allows this work to be read and, at the same time, makes such reading not a simple task.

Gwathmey Siegel's formalism has remained constant in the face of enormous stylistic changes in American architecture during the period of time considered in this essay. What ultimately defines the Gwathmey Siegel practice as both critical and formal is that the houses are not examples of individual expression, of formal integers employed stylistically to create a meaningful image. In fact, their work eschews image for other concerns, which, it will be argued here, are only appropriate to the domain of formalism. Equally, their work has little to do with the problematic concept of dwelling and the ideology of the nucleated family that occupies the single-family house. Although their work focuses on the single-family house, the style, imagery, and configuration of these houses can be understood only with reference to an evolving concern for the idea of formal type as formal process, with form seen as a dynamic, as opposed to a static, entity. While the forms are no less literally static than those of any architecture, they contain a dynamic energy similar to that of the vectored line segment. Thus any idea of type used here is to initiate a working process and is neither a justification of the traditional type nor has the idea of the reworking of typology as a goal. Rather this process attempts to empty architecture of the associations generated by the traditional categorical types. It is enough to say here that these traditional categories demanded a dialectical reading of type—i.e., figure-ground, linear-centroidal, etc.—which, in turn, suppresses other readings of the formal. While the house is the instrumentality, the institutional frame within which any architectural formalism exists, in some cases this instrumentality becomes dominant; in Gwathmey Siegel's work it becomes secondary. What makes their formalism pragmatic is that while they eschew the ideology and metaphoricity of instrumentality, their work does not seek to deny its inevitable existence.

Formal type as formal process appears over and over again in their rhetoric and is crucial to a discussion of their work. First, while this is never explicitly stated, it must be pointed out that their reference to process is linked more to the dynamic manipulation of type—to the knotting of space or the carving out of space, for example—than to the static organization of program; and second, their repeated reference to type concerns less the organization of functioning space and more the organization of these dynamic processes of form. These concerns illustrate both the strength and the limits of their work, confining it in a real way to the scale of the single-family dwelling in which both aspects operate. To discuss the formalism of their work is to discuss the question of process as type.

But what is process for Gwathmey Siegel? It is certainly not the processes of science or those analogous to linguistic phenomena. Nor is it a clearly defined transformational process, such as in the development of a cube into an extruded rectangle. Process here concerns a formal idea of space as the addition or subtraction of solid from a preexistent or ideal spatial frame. But it is particularly in the process of subtraction that a hollowing or a carving out occurs, which in itself provides the space for another kind of figural reintegration, one which deals with the problematic concepts of vector. It is this idea, in itself so anachronistic to modern architecture, that is the most interesting aspect of the Gwathmey Siegel project and that stamps with poignancy much of their early work.

In formal terms, the idea of carving usually implies a residual static form, a *poché*, which is the result of a carving out or carving away in plan and section to reveal an articulated mass. Alternatively, *modenatura*, as opposed to *poché*, was the resultant form of a type of carving in profile that traditionally provided architecture with the chiaroscuro articulation of light and shadow: *poché* was the articulation of figural form in plan; *modenatura* was the blurring of volume in section.

In American modern architecture, the closest approximations of *poché* are the plans of Wright and Kahn. But instead of a carving away one finds the concept of addition by extrusion, where the plan forms solids that can be infinitely extended vertically. There is little if no section in extruded buildings, which is why extrusion lends itself to the vertical extension of the plan into the high-rise type. It follows then that the scale of the house, as opposed to the high-rise, lends itself to the idea of hollowing out. To understand the evolution of this idea of hollowing out or carving as a vectorial process, it is not necessary to analyze systematically each building of Gwathmey Siegel in chronological sequence, but rather to focus on the houses as they begin to elaborate an alternative understanding of type.

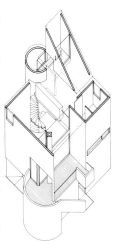

Here the rocket analogy becomes useful again to point to this other formalism, one which eludes conventional types. An initial way to use what can be called a vectorial model is to suggest two distinct categories of process. One category acts on form; the other acts on the relationship between forms and thus the position of the forms. In the former category it is possible to distinguish the following processes: aggregating, hollowing, intersecting, linear torsion, centroidal torsion, and more complex hybrids of these. In the latter category, each of these processes has a second characteristic that is either a centrifugal or a centripetal vector. Thus each of the houses will be seen to have at least one of these vectors from each category present, but often there will be two or more of these vectors present. The vector designations, as will be seen below, fall somewhere between type and process, but they do not fall into a specific physical form type, i.e., the courtyard or the eroded cube. While all of the houses may also be seen as eliciting certain of these formal types, such form categories do not adequately explain the complex activity in them. Thus these vectorial designations either fall between types or are hybrids, composites of several types.

Many of the early houses involve two of the vectorial processes. The first is a series of intersecting or interpenetrating figural volumes that have no particular concern for the form or regularity of the cubic periphery. The second of these processes implies an explosion of figural elements from an implied, originary cubic frame. These intersecting figural volumes usually have a dominant, rectilinear cubic form as the originary spatial frame with quarter- and semi-circular secondary figural volumes sometimes as circulation elements projecting from what seems to be this volumetric or vertebrate core. Sometimes other figural volumetric elements in the form of freestanding fireplaces or garage elements also project from this core. The figural elements in these projects are usually deployed on the periphery as if driven there by some centrifugal vectoring energy. The idea of this energy is common to many of the early projects.

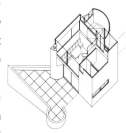

The precedent for this kind of vectoring buildup is different from most standard forms of European modernism, which derive instead from an analytic cubism that in principle relies on the subtraction of volume from or the superposition on an a priori cubic perimeter. Volumes of this European type are usually related to some form of frontal datum or vertical picture plane which places volumes in tension (extension) or compression with this planar referent. Such a layered or planar architecture is not a characteristic of Gwathmey Siegel's work. Their volumes are more akin to the haptic, non-axial volumes of van Doesburg's massing or even some of Malevich's constructivist compositions. However, even the interpenetrations of van Doesburg or Malevich produce a superposition in the internal space, where both the voided-out section and the original volume are maintained. In the Gwathmey Siegel houses these intersections become the armature for the hollowing out but do not maintain the superposition. These early houses are also different from many of their European predecessors, which were concerned with the extension and connection to other houses in rows or in sied-lungs. Equally, the simple centrifugal vector is understood to have limited use in later Gwathmey Siegel projects, where multiple and repetitive functional requirements do not allow for the action of such a vector.

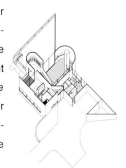

The most characteristic and seminal of the centrifugal vector houses is the Gwathmey Studio and House (*1965–67; fig. 1*). Here there is an amalgam of Le Corbusier's cubes with the sharp, angular roof forms reminiscent of the Aalsmeer House of the Dutch architects Bijvoet and Duiker and clad in the American vernacular—the vertical, untreated siding found along the New England coast. It is precisely in this juxtaposition that the denial of precedent and its concomitant ideology give way to a new vectoring of form. And with this emptying of the instrumental content comes the appearance of a formalism, a category of centrifugal vectoring.

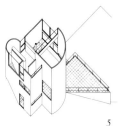

The Gwathmey House emerges from a cubic volumetric frame and explodes outward with a series of figural elements. The houses that follow from this initial model are neither as clear in their overlaying of reference nor in their purpose, but they continue to doggedly pursue variations of this vectoring process. The Straus House (*1968; fig. 2*) is an example of the kind of thematic plan variation played off the Gwathmey House. However, the sawtooth roof pieces that were fragments in the former house now become horizontal vectors, precursors of the later and important parabolic vectors. There is also here, for the first time, the appearance of an internal hollowing out, an arcing form, which is a precursor of the Steel Houses. The Sedacca House (*1968; fig. 3*) and the Cooper House (*1969*) are again variations of the explosion out from the originary frame of the Gwathmey House. The Sedacca House is interesting because it marks the first appearance of a figural element pinned in the center of the space. The stairway element, here treated without a volumetric wrapping, will become the corkscrew-like element that prefigures later work. While a variation of the Gwathmey House, the Goldberg House (*1969; fig. 4*) adds two new features. One is a raised, plinth-like terrace that becomes an extension of the sculptural massing of the central core, and the second, a volumetric extension at right angles to the core volume.

6

The Elia-Bash House (*1971–73; fig. 5*) is another of the houses evolving from the Gwathmey Studio. While it has formal elements from Richard Meier's Saltzman House and also from John Hejduk's Half House, here they are used in a conceptually, and thus formally, different manner. The house is the volumetric intersection of a quarter-circle volume with a cube and a rectangle with a half-round end. The bull-nose, quarter-round southwest corner rises above the cubic volume in section but attaches to it in plan. On the northeast corner a similar set of contrapositions occurs. What is significant about Elia-Bash is that unlike Sedacca, where the rotation is pinned off and thus carved out of a stair, or the Gwathmey Studio, where there is no internal pinning, Elia-Bash pins internally off a single column, which is simultaneously the fulcrum of the quarter-round internal volume and the horizontal wedge-shaped volume.

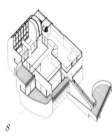

7

The Eskilson House (*1970; fig. 6*) derives from an initial cubic frame, however it is different from most centrifugal vector houses. First, in most of the early houses the torsional, figural elements are on the periphery. Here they are on the interior, the result of perhaps a centripetal action. Second, these elements are solids, as opposed to the earlier Steel Houses where they are void. Third, for the first time there is an entry portico, a freestanding, planar frontispiece that is a precursor of a theme of aggregation and then mutation and fracturing in the figural elements of the later projects. This freestanding frontispiece (which Gwathmey Siegel refer to as a *brise-soleil*) also appears in the Crowley House (*1977; fig. 7*), where it is more integrated into the main body of the house. It is important to note here that formal elements, like many of the Gwathmey Siegel icons, are usually misread as stylistic gestures rather than as formal counters in an elaborate buildup of formal energies. While style and metaphoric content can never be totally removed from any institutional setting, it is precisely their lack of development in the Gwathmey Siegel work that allows for this formal interpretation.

8

With two notable exceptions, the Sagner House (*1973; fig. 8*) is in many respects a return to the cubic-frame of the Gwathmey House. There is again a frontispiece element, which instead of being a frame or a plane, as it would have been in the case of Le Corbusier, takes the form of what only can be called an extruded volume with a quarter-round, barrel-vault roof. This sits adjacent to a half-round stairway element, which is no longer half-round in plan but only in its roof section. Second, there are internal figural elements, which are volumetric. These derive from both the Eskilson and Cogan houses, but in the context of the centrifugal vectors these elements seem anomalous.

9

While fundamentally a variation of the Gwathmey House (in fact, it is on the same site), the Tolan House (*1970; fig. 9*) adds two further components. One is the linear extension at right angles to the main volume of the house, which will evolve in later projects into a torsional vector, and the other is the walled extension of a tennis court, which is a precursor of the centripetal vectors.

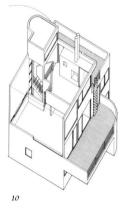

10

The Viereck House (*1979; fig. 10*) is a variation of the Gwathmey Studio with a three-story volume. The central pivot of the house is a line that connects a projecting half-round, three-story, solid stair volume in the front with a single-story, quarter-round projection in the rear. The section of this volume is sheared by the two-story volume of the porch, which intersects and carves out the primary volume. This quarter-round projection not only supports the extension of a balcony to the southeast on the middle level, but is another instance of sheared or incomplete form when compared with the half-round projection to the front. These shearing projections animate what would otherwise be a rather static three-story volume. The windows here are used to define this play of volume, both present and absent. The large square window on the upper left of the east facade plays with a similar square void underneath the projecting balcony on the lower right rear of the side facade. This, in turn, causes the void above the porch to be read as a "framed volume" even though no actual frame is present.

The Garey House (*1988; pp. 228–235*) is the last of the intersecting centrifugal vectors of the first category. The pool, instead of being inboard, is not an extension of the linear bedroom block. There are two intersecting rectilinear volumes with a three-quarter-round circular volume superposed onto the shorter rectangle.

The two Steel Houses (*1971; figs. 11, 12*) are important in the Gwathmey Siegel oeuvre because they introduce a second process, that of centripetal hollowing. Now instead of a single originary frame within an implied core, there are two frames that are seemingly rotated out of one another. The rotation suggests a knuckle or vectorial knotting in space, and thus the Steel Houses produce a series of incomplete and fragmentary arched forms. Gone is the hierarchy of an original cubic form with pendant figural accessories, and in its place emerges an irregular periphery in which the volumes are superposed and intersected, creating for the first time a plastic hollowing out of the interior. The forms are now vectors—containing the energy of a non-static, narrative record of their process of centripetal hollowing. The corkscrew-like hollowing out of the form will become the armature for the knotting of internal figural volumes that will follow. It is interesting that while in the second Steel House a cubic volume is found in a more or less secondary position in terms of the overall massing of the house, the cube is actually being cut away by the rotation of the arcing vector.

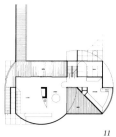

11

12

The Cohn House (*1973; fig. 13*) and the Buettner House (*1974*) are each variations of the eroded or hollowed out, as opposed to the aggregated cubic, form. What seems to define this difference is the effect of the main staircase being pulled to the center as opposed to remaining on the periphery in the aggregated cubes. The Cohn House entry is situated along a linear slot, parallel to the grain of the building. This slot is in the form of a raised bridge that penetrates a half-round circulation solid pulled forward from the main volume. This pulling forward reveals the entire front end of the cube as hollowed out. What is interesting about the Cohn House is that it marks the first appearance of a series of longitudinal striations that run parallel to the grain of the building. Three of these striations create an asymmetry, a dynamic tension, almost a torsional pull with respect to the solid perimeter: The first layer is defined by the half-round solid; the second by the extent of the second-floor balcony, which penetrates the hollowed out front; and the third is defined by the symmetrical location of the fireplace.

13

The Buettner House (*1974; fig. 14*) is typical of the centripetal process: it is a single cubic volume that is hollowed from within rather than added to from without. Here, however, the eroding energy is not from the interior stair (which is not treated as an object), but rather from the figural rotation of the double bathrooms. The house is almost Garches-like in its massing and its internal disposition. However, both cars and pedestrians enter with the grain rather than across the grain as at Garches. With the Buettner House this is not a formal problem: the volumetric graining is not an issue, save for the single frontal slot that is located by the placement of the entry stair and the freestanding object element characteristic of these early houses. However, the move to a more complex geometry and the intersection of volumes of the later houses is prefigured in this house. The cutout upper corner, reminiscent of Garches again, is done in a way that Le Corbusier would not have envisioned. The triangular, diagonally cut plane, which is resolved only by its alignment with the two horizontal windows on the south facade, prefigures the intersecting volumes of the hybrid projects of the later period. The exterior siding is now white, and there remains the ubiquitous freestanding fireplace and double-height living space opening off the kitchen area, which are formal counters of the Gwathmey Siegel houses. In fact, it might be possible to analyze the development of the centrifugal and centripetal vectoring with reference only to the formal evolution of the fireplace element. It is enough here to say that it mostly plays no role as a figural element, but rather is consistently used as a trace of some originary frame.

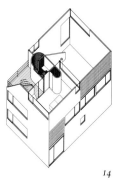

14

The Charof House (*1974; fig. 15*), like the Buettner House, is also Garches-like in its massing, particularly from the rear where there is a volumetric cutout and a stair volume extension from the main floor to the ground. The formal difference between this and Garches lies in Le Corbusier's layering of space and Gwathmey Siegel's knotting of space. Here the projecting stair element is not tied to the main volume of the house, but rather to another figural element that projects from the main cubic volume of the house. This figural projection is also tied through the volume of space to a half-round figural projection on the front of the house. Whereas in the Steel Houses the figural projections are dispersed and fragmented, here they are knotted through the main cubic volume, which acts as an armature for their deployment.

15

The Weitz and Benenson houses are seen by Gwathmey Siegel themselves as a summary of these early formal studies. The Weitz House (*1976; fig. 16*) represents the sheared and overlapped intersection of two cubic volumes, pinned by two linear extensions, front and back, which create a shearing axis. This is one of the clearest examples of the bow-tie or knot-in-space parti. The Benenson House (*1976; fig. 17*) seems from its volumetric massing to be like the Weitz House. From the exterior it has two intersecting volumes, similar to Weitz; however, on the interior these volumes are not tied together. Rather, the figural elements splay and rotate, and are centrifugal, as in the Steel Houses. It is clear that the Benenson House will lead to the Taft House by the addition of a third volume.

16

17

18

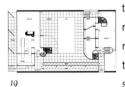

19

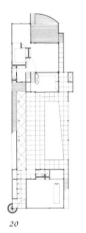

20

21

The last of the houses to begin from an irregular perimeter is the Taft House (*1977; fig. 18*). It is, in essence, three separate cubic volumes that can be read as aggregating to form a single, irregular volume. It is also possible, however, to read the parti as a single volume that is eroded to reveal either two, three, or even four parts. What is interesting about the house is a series of seeming conflicts which must be seen as intentional to this double idea of aggregating and hollowing. Thus, rather than three arbitrary, floating elements, they can be seen as a suspension, hovering between these two types of vectors.

While the earliest houses were both aggregating, intersecting, and hollowing, a later group of houses can be seen as predominantly hollowing. Unlike the earlier houses, which have an irregular perimeter, these houses begin from an idea of a fixed, enclosing, rectilinear perimeter, which is then eroded or eaten away by a centripetal, internalizing vector to create an enclosed, exterior volume. In traditional, formal typological terms, these would be seen as courtyard houses. However, here again the centripetal action inherent in these houses is not accounted for in such a static classification. The first of these—the Geffen House (*1973; fig. 19*) is the model—is linear in its site plan, with two lateral volumes closing the front and back of the site with a hollowed out open volume, or "court," of space in the center. This type has its historical precedents in Le Corbusier's houses for Dr. Currutchet in La Plata, Argentina, and the Sarabhai House in Ahmedabad, India. Both the Geffen House and the Block House follow this essential parti type.

It is interesting that these enclosed perimeter houses do not follow the volumetric massing of the first category of a volumetric aggregation, but instead begin to introduce a plaid striation of layered space. In this they still bear little relationship to their modern precursors, Mies van der Rohe's court houses, which are more about pinwheeling, articulate volumes than they are about layered space. In the Geffen House there is the first articulated, two-story frontal screen in Gwathmey Siegel's work. This, along with the ramped courtyard parti, clearly resonates with Le Corbusier's Currutchet House. However, here the entry is not through the screen itself but rather through a slot on the southeast corner. In fact, the section through the ramp is more reminiscent of Le Corbusier's villa at Poissy than it is of La Plata. A regular grid of round columns provides a field for the curvilinear figural forms of the bath, storage, fireplace, and stairs, confirming this reminiscence of Poissy. While Gwathmey Siegel say that this house is a hybrid between a courtyard and the row-house type of Garches, there is too much of the figural object qualities of Poissy in section and plan for the latter reading to be sustained. Yet it is just the idea of the hybrid, the heterogeneous mixing of formal types, that will become central to Gwathmey Siegel's work.

The Block House project (*1979; fig. 20*) is another of the enclosed perimeter houses with two volumes connected by a long, linear volume. Again, it is an elongated version of the Dr. Currutchet project in La Plata. It presents a garage frontispiece and a long, enclosing ramp on its eastern side. Here the idea of carving out is clearly articulated. At the northeast corner a circular stair articulated as a solid cylinder is let into the corner, fracturing it and creating not so much a series of planes (because the volume is still visually attached to the frontispiece) as an intersection of volumes. There exists within and without a series of symmetries both partial and whole.

In several of these fixed perimeter schemes there is a central or dominant axis that is subjected to linear torsional forces on the interior. In many cases the single bar becomes either a series of volumetric spatial slices deployed parallel to the longitudinal axis or a series of volumetric pavilions. In either case, what distinguishes them is that they are no longer hollowing even though there is a centripetal action. This centripetal action of the stair acts mainly to produce torsion along a central spine, which then fractures the formal elements themselves.

The clearest of these houses is the Cogan House (*1977; fig. 21*). Here, three major landforms are shaped: the pool, the terrace, and the lawn. None are treated volumetrically. Thus, the house itself is a single, longitudinal volume spanning the short dimension of the site. This volume is penetrated across its grain (and along the grain of the site) by a second, lower volume that marks the entry in front and defines the outside terrace in the rear. This linear crossing is imploded by a bull-nosed bathroom element on the lowest level and exploded by a circular stair that continues through all three levels. Together, these two pieces act to hollow out the space of the crossing at the lower level. However, this crossing is twisted on the second and third levels by a double-height volume that extends this vector along the main axis of the space. A second torsional element, characteristic of many of these enclosed partis, is the internal ramp extending parallel along the front plane of the volume and providing access to the public living space on the upper level.

The Haupt House (*1976; fig. 22*) also has a curious parti. In many respects it could easily be seen as either aggregated from an elongated cube or as hollowed out from an enclosing perimeter. This latter reading is possible since the pool, which is in a raised platform, creates a court-like enclosure covalent with the main periphery of the house. However, it is against such a literalist interpretation of static massing that this essay is directed; such readings deny the fundamental validity of the Gwathmey Siegel work. It is only when their formalism is read as formal processes that the projects take on their full value. Thus the Haupt House must be seen as a torsional line deriving from its major circulation element, which is a linear ramp.

22

The deMenil House (*1979; fig. 23*) in East Hampton also has an enclosing frame, but the vectorial energy is aggregating rather than hollowing. Made of three linear volumes or striations, the house, because of the dominance of the two enclosing bars, has qualities of compressive centrifugal energy. In fact, the central segment is composed of figural elements that are linked like beads on a string from the second-level balcony to the left of the glass screen on the front facade, to the stair that penetrates out and down from the central zone into the rear *brise-soleil* area.

23

The Opel House (*1985; pp. 244–253*) is articulated differently than any of the Gwathmey Siegel houses. It is neither an enclosed frame nor an aggregated parti, but rather contains elements of both along a torsional spine. The house derives from the Row House project (*1979*) submitted to the IAUS "Idea as Model" exhibition in 1979. It also has roots in the Hines House project of the same year. This is a crucial house because it marks a significant departure from any vector as defined by a circulation element, whether it be a stair or a ramp. Instead, the vector is defined by the roof element. In fact, the most significant element in this project is the parabolic roof form. While the authors themselves would acknowledge this as a clever way to overcome local codes that did not allow flat roofs, without capitulating to the pitched-roof syndrome, there is much more at work in this idea. The parabolic roof form implies a new category of hollowed out space, one which is not merely centripetal in plan, but simultaneously torsionally extruded in section. This category of extrusion derives from Arata Isozaki's prefiguration of a new spatial typology that emerges with his first use of the barrel vault in his museum projects in the early 1970s—the horizontal linear extrusion that could bend and turn, and thus deny both the free-plan space of early modernism and its latter incarnation in the development of parallel, cross-wall partis.

The Steinberg House (*1986–89; pp. 254–263*) is a house in transition. In a sense it begins an idea of a composite house. Even though many of the houses exhibit multiple characteristics, the composite house is one in which the formal elements themselves no longer define the object; the composite is made up of disparate formal elements. While much of the Steinberg House is defined by the single dominant and linear barrel vault, which creates a torsional vector, other pieces fall outside its enclosure. As different from the aggregating and hollowing vectors, the torsional vector comes from vaulted forms that do not derive their formal energy from the plans but rather from the section. And since most of Gwathmey Siegel's volumetric development comes from the plan, these roof forms become somewhat anomalous. In the Steinberg House there is a series of three linear volumetric layers, extruded longitudinally, that follow from the deMenil parti of Long Island. There are two narrow circulation layers on either side of a central volume, which is partially covered over its length by an extruded, half-round vault. This causes the central volume to be read as a linear spine with a series of figural volumes projecting from it. The plan organization is a series of cross-wall divisions that compartmentalize the central space into a sequence of utilitarian divisions bearing little relationship to the barrel-vaulted section. That there are clearly formal energies at work can be seen from the exterior massing. From the west end the tripartite, horizontally extruded parti is clearly dominant, although there are two figural projections, a half-round balcony on the southwest and a two-story curved volumetric expansion on the northwest, confounding this reading. To the east there is no sectional reading at all. It is as if there had been a collision or a rupture somewhere along the central axis. Thus, only when these formal energies become intentional, when they lead to some *other,* third condition, can a house truly be said to be a composite that has few precedents in the formal history of residential architecture. However, these hybrids will be seen to be the most original and thus significant in the Gwathmey Siegel oeuvre. They occur in the later houses because, as the projects become larger (as is the case with most successful practices), the partis become, of necessity, more elaborated. Now, instead of juxtaposing formal elements in a single parti, the parti itself becomes a transformational element, a counter in a continual internalization of the formal development. These hybrids cannot be defined by merely noting aggregating or hollowing vectors, for they pose more complex formal issues. They are the most successful when they remain close to the original Gwathmey Siegel parti strategies, that is, when they are seen as a formal development in plan and when there are no iconic elements, such as gratuitous oculi windows, to confuse their intention.

The first deMenil House (*1979; fig. 24*), in Houston, Texas, is one of the earliest of the composite houses. This is partly due to the circumstances that required the incorporation of an existing structure. What Gwathmey Siegel did was to create

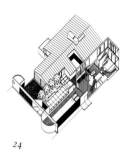

24

25

a frontispiece, essentially made up of a dropped, deep beam supported on a series of volumes that extend from the front of this plane and simultaneously seem to be pulled to the rear. Thus, the open space between the two volumes is interstitial rather than residual. It can be seen to be created both by aggregation and by erosion of the volume by a pool that cuts into the space. This bivalent vectoring is one characteristic of these hybrid houses.

The second of these composite houses is the Gimelstob House (*1982; fig. 25*). Initially the parti would seem to be a hollowed center, particularly when seen from the inside. However, the northwest corner is eroded away, revealing a series of three blocks that are aggregated together. The first of these volumes, a north-facing block, is horizontal with a parabolic extruded roof section that again suggests a linear torsional energy. A second rectilinear block is articulated slightly lower than the first, yet intersecting its corner. The third block is a thickened wall plane rendered in red terra-cotta to create a ground or plinth. This is the first time a plinth is so articulated in a Gwathmey Siegel project. It acts both as a ground datum and as a volumetric element because of its coloring, which is different from that of the lateral volumes. However, the idea of a plinth as a formal type is denied by an erosion of its southeast corner by a two-story block. In the main volume there is a curious play in plan between a Palladian villa with two wings set about an axial fireplace and an asymmetric entry reminiscent of the binuclear house plans of Gropius and Breuer. Is this irresolution or purposeful ambiguity? Because of the strength of the parabolic roof, which spans continuously over both possible readings, one is forced to conclude that neither of these formalist-type readings is intended. But this is not a persuasive explanation. It becomes so only when an assumed modernism understood as a homogeneous formal vocabulary is proposed for the work. This assumption is made all the more plausible because of the overriding modern vocabulary that seems to link the early work with the later. But it would seem that the movement from plan generation to horizontal sectional development is more than just a movement away from modernism. Indeed, it suggests a radically different view of composition. The idea of a holistic order, or an inside-outside integration, of a "plan generator," is denied. Instead, there is a movement to aggregational and torsional vectors, not as compositional elements, as in the earlier schemes, but as displaced by a more casual, haptic compositional attitude that is guided neither by programmatic necessity nor by an overriding aesthetic ideal. Now composition is more like a juxtaposition of ready-made parts that say nothing to each other or to the idea of the whole. This silence now illuminates the mute formalism of these fragments qua fragments as their only condition of being.

The Bechtler House (*1993; pp. 278–283*) in Switzerland again can be seen initially to have a European parti evolving from the binuclear houses of Walter Gropius and ultimately the parti of the Bauhaus in Dessau. This parti is then overlaid in the main block with a striated version of Frank Lloyd Wright's Martin House grid. The parti is thus initially compositional, but in a composite manner combines aspects of both courtyard and binuclear houses at its entry level. The plan presents a single Palladian volume with two seemingly symmetrical entries in slots flanking the central volume. One slot is indeed an entry, while the other slot is for through circulation. As in all of the later projects, there is a disjunction between plan and section that precludes any vertical extrusion from the plan. Rather, a barrel- or parabolic-vaulted roof section is present. But here it is also fragmented, split in two, running across and counter to the grain of the plan striations. The barrel vaults themselves are split and sheared into two parabolic segments over the main volume of the house and a third parabolic segment over the service volume. Unlike most Gwathmey Siegel projects the house is cut into a sloping site. Thus the entry is at an upper mid-level.

There are two wings parallel to the slope of the ground and one wing perpendicular to these wings, which connects to them in such a way as to act as a fulcrum for the pair of seemingly sheared bars moving in opposite directions. There is an asymmetrical play in the composite imbalance on the front facade; the fenestration of the side block is centered, while the fenestration of the central block is asymmetrical. These are clearly compositional gestures. And one of the problems that gradually becomes evident in these larger houses is that the impulse to control the often haptic nature of the vectorial movements often devolves into a desire for compositional control.

The Chen House in Taipei (*1989; pp. 284–291*) is also an anachronism among Gwathmey Siegel houses; it is vertically massed and reminiscent of Richard Meier's Smith or Douglas houses. Here, as in most Gwathmey Siegel houses, there is an internal formal referencing. The section is the most significant; rising out of a subterranean, three-story drum, it is a conning tower–like series of volumes, cantilevering from a central stair core. The house is thus difficult to classify because its torsional energy is uniquely vertical, rising out of the ground like a corkscrew out of a bottle. The house is bounded on four sides by built walls that extend up from a plinth containing four underground levels of service and ancillary functions.

The above-grade plan is a four-level vertical block, one end of which has a series of sculpted forms and the other end a series of volumes that step out and away from the main block. In fact, from the rear corner the house is reminiscent of Adolf Loos's Steiner House in Vienna. In elevation and in plan the house is striated from left to right by a solid stair volume, an entry slot that reads as a void, and a second slot. Each of these parts forms a very delicate subtext of symmetrical and asymmetrical rhythms. For example, the right-most living room bay is divided into a symmetrical "ABA" tripartite scheme in the middle two floors of the facade. It is split into two asymmetrical solid-void parts, echoing a similar split that occurs in the rear of the plan with the stepped back (in section) projections, which again split the living room volume in two. But the living room volume is also sheared by the axis of symmetry about the two freestanding circular columns. Another axis, this time from above, created by the symmetry of the children's bedrooms, again cleaves the living room in a second axis of symmetry. These dissonant axes demand to be read as what they are—formal fragments with no single meaning. Here the house clearly empties out response to historic precedent, functional program, structure, aesthetics, and meaning. One is left a response that can only be to the formal.

The Oceanfront House (*1988; pp. 268–277*) is another example of a large house whose compositional strategies are consistently denied on both the exterior and interior volumes. Here there is a hollowing within a hollowing. First, the containing enclosure is broken in the front by three different-sized striations that course against the grain of the site from front to back, and east to west. These striations also shear the plane of a frontal volume as they move through it. There is a frontal interior court that is, in turn, crossed by an asymmetric vector from the entry. This vector sets up a series of asymmetric volumetric plays. The front, or inboard, side of the house is articulated subtly by three almost unpunctuated volumetric planes that seem to slide loosely in front of each other, from right to left. The presence of two alternating raised plinths further divides these volumes into four. The corner of the left-most edge is undercut by the presence of two garage doors, while the right-most edge is slightly beveled. Each of these registers of form countermands any single idea. Rather they suggest a multiple order that is enfolded centripetally on the interior. On the outboard side a screen fence and a raised plinth are the only indications of a unifying court. Once inside this perimeter, the house becomes a series of articulated pavilions, seemingly aggregated and thus appearing to contradict the centripetal vector.

Architecture, unlike any other discourse, is prisoner of its institutional frame, and it is this that defines its instrumentality. This is most clearly the case in the individual dwelling, which has defined more than any other building category the social structure of its inhabitants. It can be argued that the gable-roofed, single-family, detached house of the American suburb has contributed more to the social and political institution of the nucleated family than any other comparable institution. It was this institutional frame that was attacked, with very little success, by the flat-roofed, machine-image ideology of the modern houses of Le Corbusier. Within these structures the program of bourgeois life remained virtually intact. While its symbolism of shelter, comfort, and enclosure may have been altered, the structure of the institution of middle-class life remained. This is because the institutional frame of architecture, unlike most other discourses, cannot be dislodged by style or ideology. This is also true for architectural formalism; except for several moments in its history, architectural formalism has been difficult to displace. In fact, formalism, it can be argued, is the only condition of architecture that can displace its own disciplinary frame. What is so interesting about the work of Gwathmey Siegel is that it neither challenges nor denies this institutional frame.

The trajectory of the architectural rocket, no matter how much the launchers may wish it to be otherwise, always falls back into the same place, that is, to its own metaphysic: construction, walls, doors, openings, and the like. To their credit, Gwathmey and Siegel have never claimed otherwise. Their work merely says that architecture will always be within the home and proceeds from there. Quite simply, the iconography of their housing has nothing to do with the home. In its tacit acceptance of home (it makes no claims on either side of the argument of habitation versus occupation) it reuses both European modernism and New England puritanism, both morals and manners. This is the crucial distinction in their work that animates the entire house-project oeuvre. They have managed to launch their work into a trajectory, no matter how grand or how modest, that has inevitably fallen close to the site of a formalism derived from the philosophical tenets of American pragmatism. It is a consistent restrategizing of formalism, which has its roots in the very pragmatism of their work, that allows us to read their work not as style or ideology, but simply as architecture.

earlier work, from top: 1969 Dormitory, Dining, and Student Union Building, SUNY Purchase; 1970 Whig Hall, Princeton University; 1976 East Campus Student Housing and Academic Center, Columbia University; 1979 Library and Science Building, Westover Schoo

Educational/Arts Buildings and Projects

detail of west and north facades showing intersection of addition and monitor building

New York, New York
1982–1992

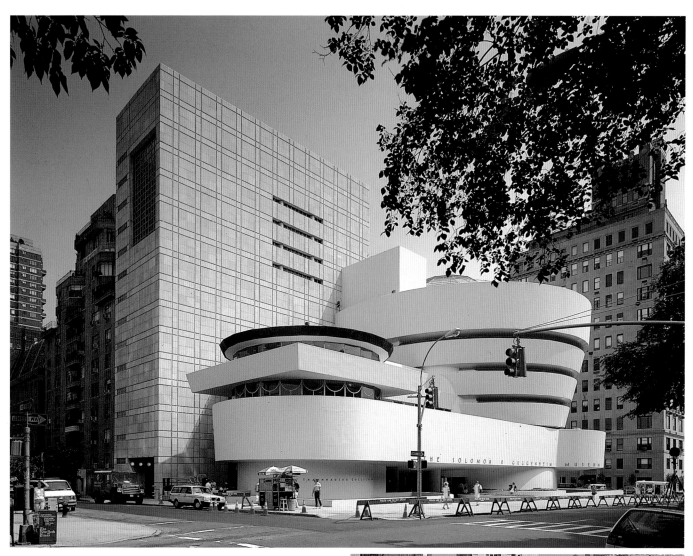

Guggenheim Museum Addition

top: northwest view from Fifth Avenue, bottom: aerial view from Central Park

In 1981, we were asked by the president of the trustees and the director of the Solomon R. Guggenheim Museum to evaluate the institution's building, site, and programmatic potential as it approached the twenty-first century. The year-and-a-half study documented the original Frank Lloyd Wright building, the history of its previous, partially realized additions, and its zoning limitations and provided a comprehensive program analysis and suggestions for alternative expansion possibilities.

Our first scheme was a constructivist assemblage that engaged the original building with a strong intervention, thereby recasting the museum's bilateral asymmetry into a tripartite composition. In the spirit of Wright's original, subversively contextual intervention, we proposed a contextually contrapuntal addition, intended to challenge common perceptions about the existing building and site.

Public and critical reaction, coming on the heels of Michael Graves's first proposal for an addition to the Whitney Museum of American Art, was primarily negative. Preservation groups, neighborhood activists, and Frank Lloyd Wright loyalists, including Taliesen West, established a formidable and organized opposition, with the architectural historian Edgar Kaufmann Jr. as the leading spokesperson.

Approval for the addition was required by the New York Board of Standards and Appeals, which traditionally addresses only legal and zoning variances, not aesthetics. However, the controversy and high profile of this project influenced the board, for the first time in its history, to base its findings on both legal and aesthetic judgments. Following Kaufmann's eloquent, preservationist presentation, the board rejected our initial scheme. We then proposed an alternative that was less aggressive as an object in conflict with the museum and more referential—and reverential—to Frank Lloyd Wright's original vision of an annex as a background wall to the north, four-story monitor building. Despite continued presentations—often irrational and inaccurate—by the opposition, the second scheme received the board's approval in 1986, helped in part by Edgar Kaufmann's endorsement.

Shortly thereafter, Thomas Krens succeeded Thomas Messer as the Guggenheim director and initiated a new vision for the institution, which included building annex museums around the world. His expansion plans resulted in a positive and dramatic programmatic and architectural reevaluation of the original Guggenheim and the proposed addition. Nearly all of the ancillary functions, including art storage, conservation, and library resources, would be moved off-site, thus freeing 90 percent of the space for the public exhibition of art. Krens's proposal resolved a longstanding conflict between the Guggenheim's goals and its space limitations; it freed the institution, philosophically and literally, to fulfill its primary and historical mission as a modern avant-garde exhibition museum.

wall detail on Fifth Avenue, mid-block

Frank Lloyd Wright originally intended the large rotunda and adjacent two-story gallery to be the only exhibition spaces. The monitor building was to accommodate administrative, library, and other related functions. The two opposing spatial organizations—the ascending spiral ramp and domed skylight of the rotunda, and the horizontally stacked "prairie house" pavilions of the monitor building—were internally separated. However, when the Thannhauser Collection was donated in 1954, the second floor of the monitor building was renovated as permanent gallery space, which established the precedent for spatial interconnection between the monitor building and the large rotunda. We extended this precedent by converting each floor of the monitor building into exhibition-gallery space and by integrating the pavilions, functionally and spatially, with the large rotunda.

The parti for the addition was determined by its juncture with the existing circulation core. Intersecting with the full cycle plan of each ramp at the elevator and triangular stair landing, the new form provides balcony views and access to three new two-story galleries (on levels two and three, five and six, and seven and eight) and one single-story gallery (on the fourth level). The large rotunda thus becomes the courtyard-cloister space for the new addition as well as for the monitor building, where four distinct and interconnected horizontal pavilions offer views to Central Park and to the skylighted small rotunda, an eloquent counterpoint to the large rotunda spiral. Unique views of the original Wright building are also visible from the new galleries, as segments of the covered east facade have been reexposed in both section and elevation.

The two critical intersections between the original building and the addition reinforce the memory of the autonomous monitor building. They occur internally around the triangular stair, which is now experienced both as a space and as an object, and at the transparent glass wall between the addition and the monitor building, which reveals the original facades from the outside in and the inside out. Externally, the new fifth-floor roof sculpture terrace, the large rotunda roof terrace, and the renovated public ramp from the street to the auditorium reveal the original building in a new and comprehensive perspective.

top: neighborhood context on Eighty-ninth Street, bottom: new entry and service gates

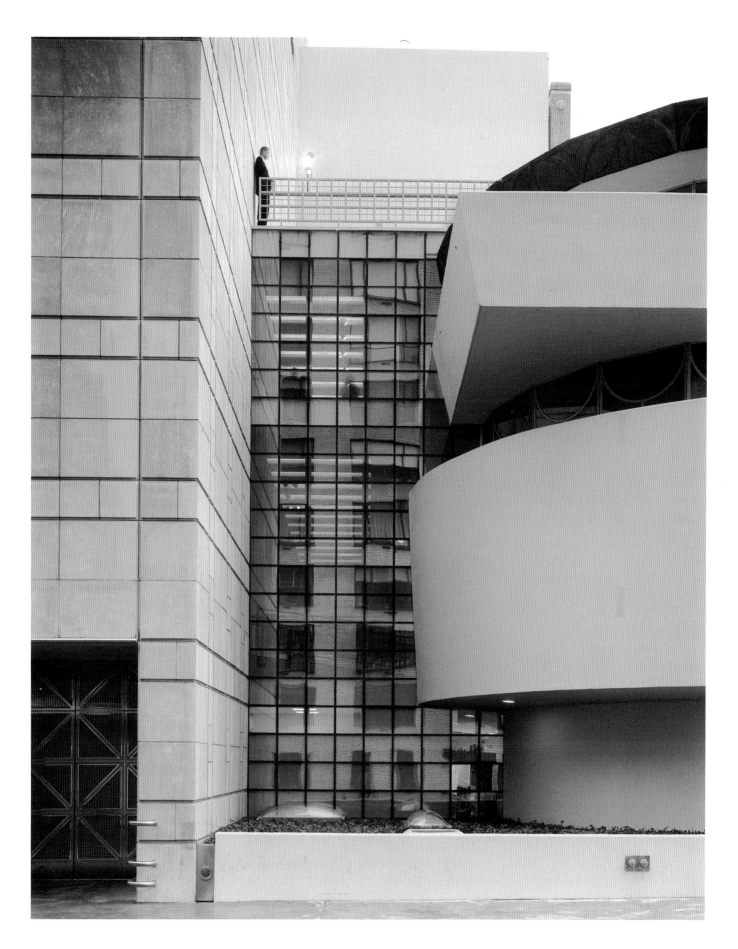

detail of north facade showing glass wall between addition and monitor building

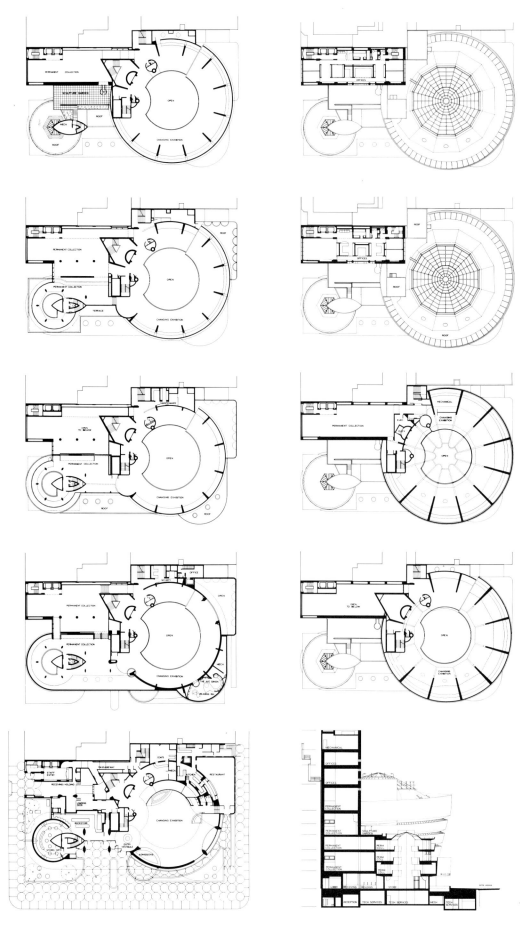

bottom left to top right: ground-level through ninth-level plans, bottom right: section through addition and monitor building

23

new second- and third-level gallery with Thannhauser gallery beyond

renovated Thannhauser gallery on second level of monitor building

new second- and third-level gallery from third-level balcony of monitor building

fourth-level gallery in monitor building with reconstituted Frank Lloyd Wright cornice

top: renovated fourth level of the monitor building with view toward Central Park, bottom: view north through glass connecting wall

new fourth-level gallery with fourth level of monitor building beyond

new fifth- and sixth-level gallery with access to new roof terrace

top: new roof terrace showing intersection of large rotunda and addition, bottom left: terrace outside large rotunda, bottom right: terrace railings and small rotunda skylight

top and bottom: north stair of addition

renovated seventh-level ramp in large rotunda

new seventh- and eighth-level gallery

top: director's office and boardroom with view north, bottom: conference area on the administrative level with view west

typical workstation with view west over Central Park reservoir

newly renovated Fifth Avenue ramp with entry to auditorium

Closed to the public since the museum's inception, the seventh-floor ramp of the rotunda has also been renovated to provide a culmination of the exhibition space for the first time. The extension of the last ramp into the final double-height gallery of the new addition formally rectifies the former dead-end experience and also provides an essential alternative circulation route back to the ground floor.

It is hoped that the design process and the completed addition will reveal that there is more to preservation than maintaining what exists. Our particular preservationist ethic was not only to save the original, but in the spirit of archaeological discovery, to enrich the spatial experience while maintaining the architectural integrity of Wright's vision.

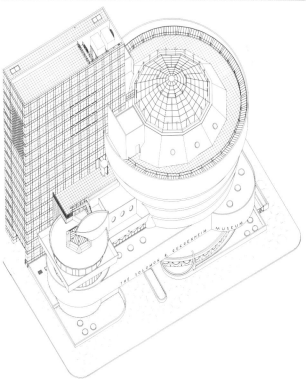

top: south facade of addition from roof of large rotunda, bottom: axonometric of project

Astoria, New York
1983–1988

Housed in a landmark three-story loft building adjacent to the Astoria motion pictures studio complex, the museum is both an archive-repository and a learning center for movie and video history where exhibits are designed to encourage hands-on exploration.

Program flexibility requirements and a limited budget determined the primary aesthetic and construction phasing. The permanent ground-floor intervention includes a flexible exhibition gallery, state-of-the-art 200-seat movie theater, bookstore-museum shop, lobby, and café. The second floor houses administrative offices, a multiuse exhibition loft, and the Tut's Fever Movie Palace. Designed by artist Red Grooms as an interpretation of Egyptian-style movie theaters of the twenties and thirties, Tut's theater adds an engaging dynamic to the exhibition content. The third floor is a multiuse exhibition loft, and the roof will accommodate a prefabricated metal pavilion, providing exhibition and entertainment space.

A new monumental stair and elevator tower was placed on axis with the main entrance to the building, extending from the original courtyard facade as a counterpoint to the gridded solid-void frame of the facade. The stair is the iconic object of the design and the orientation element for the entire complex. The landings provide visitors with an alternative exhibition experience and an opportunity to reorient themselves before reentering through the facade of the original building, creating a sense of anticipation and reengagement. In the final phase, the courtyard will be developed as an outdoor movie theater and exhibition space to hold larger-scale installations.

American Museum of the Moving Image

top: landmark facade of renovated building, bottom: building before renovation

new stair tower viewed from courtyard

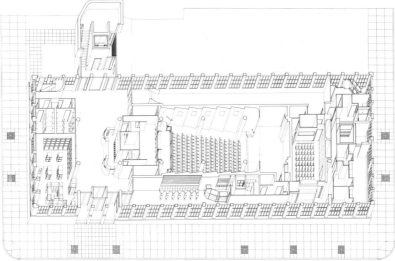

top: museum entry, bottom: axonometric plan of ground level

museum shop from lobby

left and right: two views of new stair tower from courtyard

left: interior of stair, right: ground level of multiuse exhibition loft

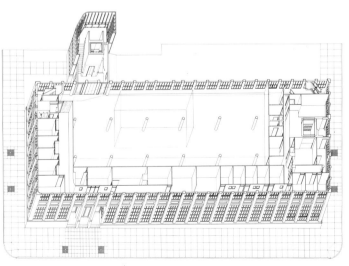

top: new 200-seat movie theater, bottom left: Red Grooms's Tut's Fever Movie Palace on second level, bottom right: axonometric plan of second level

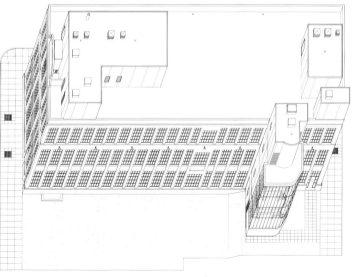

top: typical exhibition gallery on second level, bottom: axonometric of building exterior

Hanover, New Hampshire
1984–1988

The program called for an expansion of the athletic facilities housed in the original Alumni Gymnasium, a generic 1910 structure of brick and granite with a cross-axial plan and pitched roof. The new building, flanked by two sets of tennis courts, is adjacent to athletic fields and a residential street. The ground floor includes three basketball courts with bleacher seating that extends to define an intercollegiate competition court, a physical-fitness center and classroom, varsity locker rooms, athletic ticket offices, and a concession area. The second floor, reached by two stairs

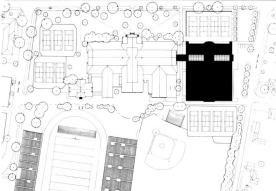

and a bridge from the Alumni Gymnasium, houses seven competition squash courts, racquetball courts, a dance studio, and spectator bleacher balconies, all accessed from a barrel-vaulted, skylighted gallery terminated by a bay window overlooking the street and entry below.

Horizontal and vertical circulation elements wrap three sides of the basketball arena, allowing natural light on the north facade into the fitness center and dance studio, as well as articulating the building's interior activities. In abstract counterpoint to the existing gymnasium, the exterior materials—brick, ground-face concrete block, cast stone, and painted wood windows—address contextual constraints while articulating the hierarchical, volumetric, and layered organization of the plan.

John Berry Sports Center, Dartmouth College

top: northeast corner from lawn and tennis courts, bottom: site plan

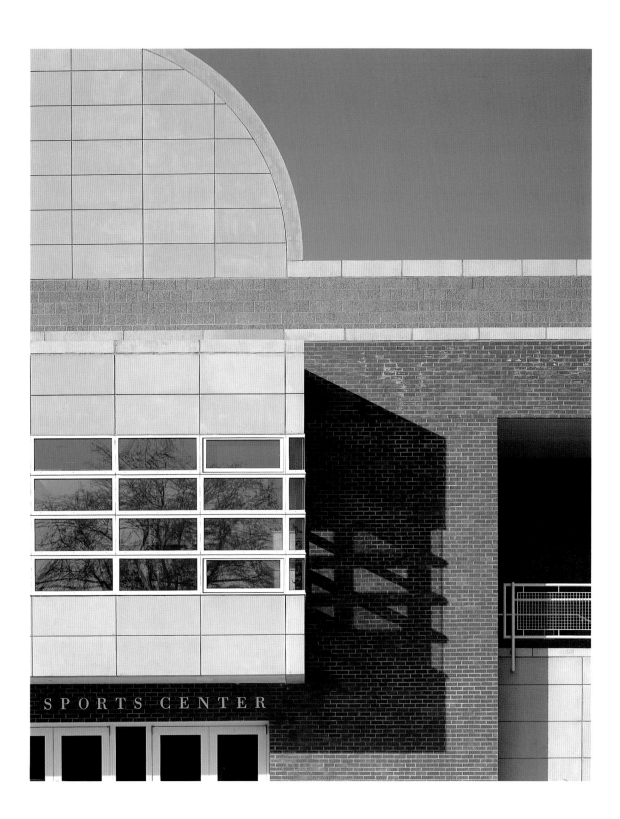

detail of gallery bay window above public entry

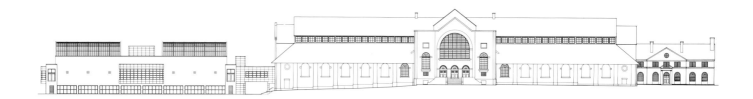

top: south facade from practice fields and tennis courts, bottom: north elevation of Sports Center and Alumni Gymnasium

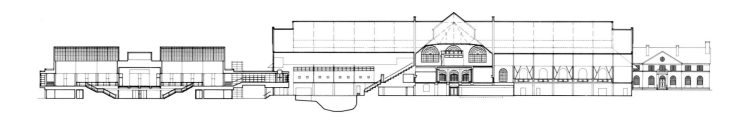

top: night view of north facade from tennis courts, bottom: section through Sports Center and Alumni Gymnasium

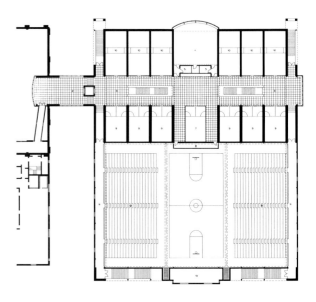

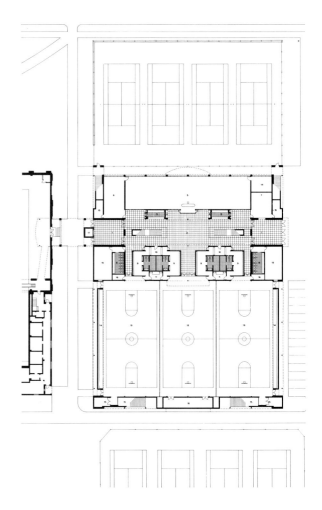

left: basketball arena from spectator balcony, right: ground-level and gallery-level plans

basketball arena

spectator gallery for squash courts showing stair from lobby and bay window at end of gallery

left: spectator gallery with bridge beyond, right: three-glass-wall exhibition squash court

Ithaca, New York
1984–1990

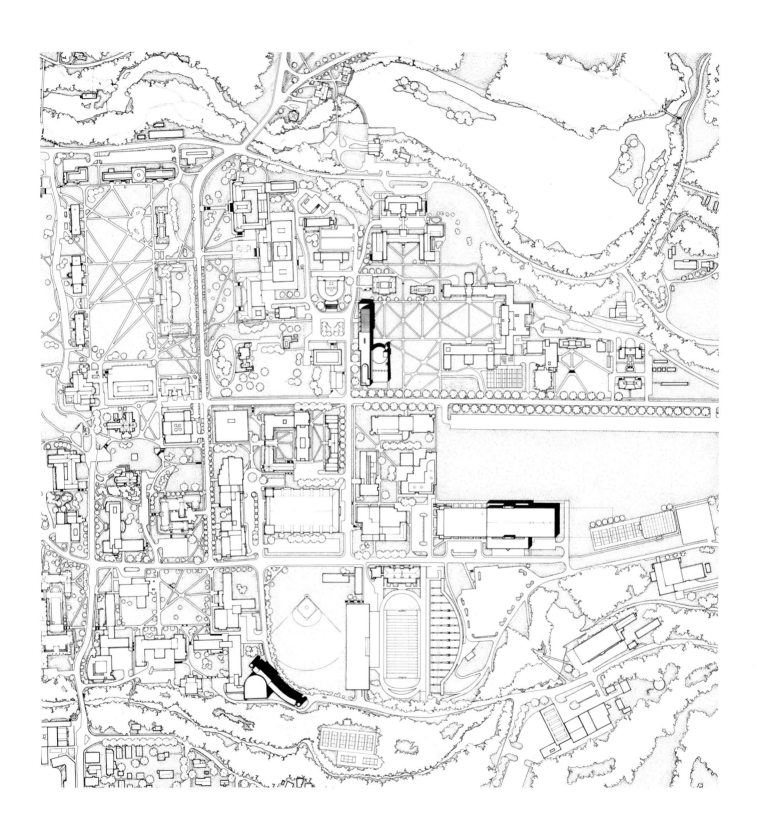

Cornell University Buildings

site plan of north campus

At the time we began these three projects, the president of Cornell University, Frank Rhodes, was critical of many recent buildings on campus and had become the leading advocate for a new architectural sensibility and awareness. At our recommendation, the dean and a faculty member from the School of Architecture were appointed for the first time to the Cornell Architectural Review Committee.

All three buildings on the north campus—the School of Agriculture, the Fieldhouse and Basketball Arena, and the Theory Center at the College of Engineering—share common elements. They are larger than adjacent buildings, they address the issue of edge and define major outdoor spaces, and they establish precedents for a master plan that supports the urban constraints and constructs of each site. Constructive interaction with the user groups, the facilities planners, and the administration was essential to the realization of these projects.

The School of Agriculture building closes the quadrangle at the end of its west axis. It forms a gateway from the south campus to Bailey Plaza, which has been redefined as an outdoor pedestrian court that anchors the main campus auditorium and adjacent structures. The Fieldhouse and Basketball Arena is an addition to the hockey rink that redefines the edge of the practice fields at the center of the north campus. The Theory Center is contextually more complex than the other two buildings, as it borders a gorge that posed significant ecological constraints. It is located on the curve of Campus Road, facing the baseball field, and is diagonally opposite the football stadium and the existing fieldhouse, the two largest structures on campus.

With the completion of the three buildings, a precedent for Cornell University architecture was realized: site responsive, programmatically flexible, materially dense and scale-sensitive buildings. In their formal articulation, contextual interaction, and use of collage, these new structures are intended to read simultaneously as extensions and transformations.

top: School of Agriculture from quadrangle, middle: Fieldhouse and Basketball Arena from Schoellkopf Field, bottom: Theory Center from Campus Road

Ithaca, New York
1984–1989

School of Agriculture, Cornell University

A user-intensive reevaluation of a previously rejected scheme for the site initiated the design process for the School of Agriculture. The rejected design, basically a mid-rise office building, was insensitive to specific site and program constraints.

Open-ended on the long (west) axis facing Bailey Plaza, the Agriculture quadrangle was defined by five-story masonry buildings on three sides. The new Administrative building, fronting both Bailey Plaza and the Agriculture quad, redefines Bailey Plaza as an urban space, and the quadrangle as an enclosed outdoor room. The building houses administrative offices on the first three floors and the Landscape Architecture School on the fourth floor. Crowning the building is a barrel-vaulted studio space with double-height windows facing the quadrangle and a framed roof terrace facing Bailey Plaza. A connecting bridge provides access to the Landscape department from the Academic building and frames a three-story gate to the quadrangle that recalls similar college gates on the campus.

A primary pedestrian pathway from the quadrangle to the campus, the gate forms one of the main entrances to the Academic building; the other is at the corner of Tower Road and Garden Avenue. A two-story galleria with a balcony mezzanine is the primary interior circulation space, connecting the two entrances and providing access to classrooms, a 600-seat lecture auditorium, and a 400-seat dining facility. The third and fourth floors of the building house faculty offices and teaching-support space.

On the exterior, modular brick in three shades of earth tones recalls the texture of adjacent campus buildings. The windows are teak, with cast-stone sills and copings, and the barrel-vaulted roof is standing-seam lead-coated copper. This 140,000-square-foot, four-story building addresses the pertinent issues of a major college structure —context, material, scale, and image—in a manner that supports both a new program and the traditions of the school.

east facade from quadrangle

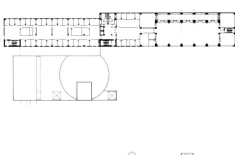
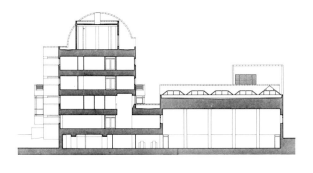

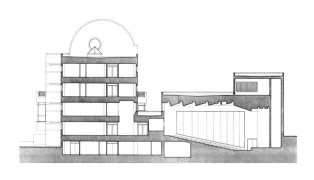
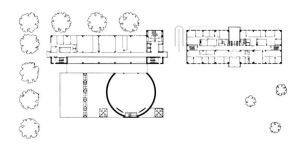
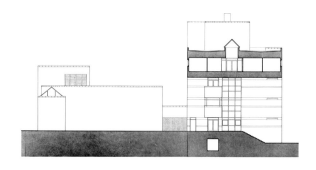
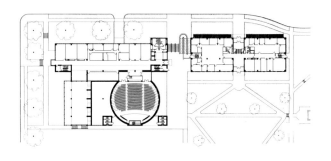
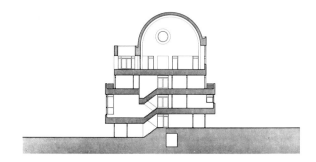
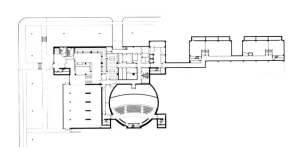

plans, from bottom: basement, ground level, second level, third level, fourth level, sections, from bottom: through Administrative building, entry-gate bridge, auditorium, and dining hall

top: entry gate from Bailey Plaza, bottom left: circulation gallery in Academic building, bottom right: stair and student lounge in Administrative building

Landscape Architecture studio

61

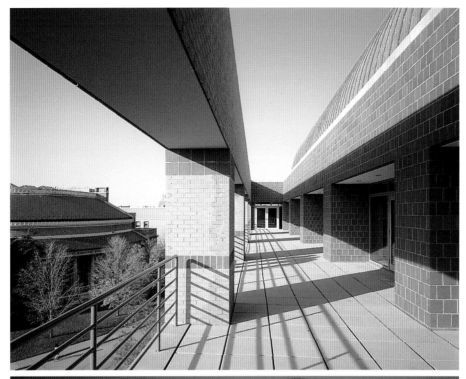

top: Landscape Architecture studio terrace overlooking Bailey Plaza, bottom: dean's office overlooking quadrangle

top: dining hall from graduate student lounge, bottom left: detail of dining hall skylight, bottom right: 600-seat auditorium

entry to Academic building from Tower Road

Ithaca, New York
1985–1989

Fieldhouse and Basketball Arena, Cornell University

north facade from practice fields

top: entry arcade, bottom: main stair

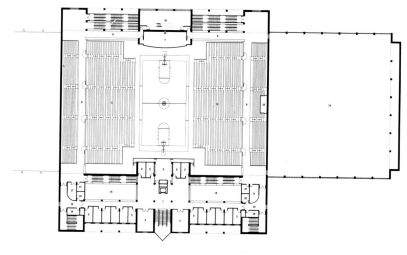

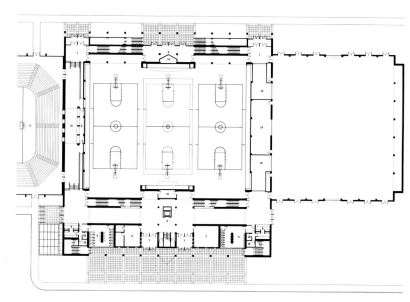

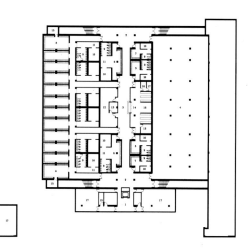

Forming the southern edge of Cornell's varsity practice fields, the Fieldhouse and Basketball Arena establishes a new image for athletic facilities on campus. Future plans include a natatorium and indoor tennis courts to the east that will complete the southern built edge, recognizing and reinforcing the quadrangle's historical role as a referential outdoor space in campus architecture.

The building comprises two major volumes: a basketball arena with three regulation NCAA courts and roll-out seating for 5,000 spectators, and the fieldhouse-cage. The three courts merge to form a single exhibition court when the two-tiered bleachers are extended. A continuous balcony surrounds the arena at the upper-bleacher level. At one end, an alumni lounge overlooks the court through a bay window; at the other end are coaches' offices. The balcony volumes create an object-frame notation, transforming the scale of the arena walls. The cage is a large, naturally lit multipurpose sports practice space that includes a climbing wall for teaching and training.

Circulation spaces layer the exterior, creating recessed porches and covered entrances for pedestrians on the north and south facades. Symmetrical, monumental stairs on the north porch mirror interior stairs in the two-story skylighted lobby. The lobby is the organizational fulcrum of the building, linking the office-service areas with the main athletic spaces and providing an interconnecting public entrance to the hockey rink. The circulation spaces, lobby, and stairs intersect with the playing volumes to evoke a sense of anticipation and expectation upon arrival.

Whereas most of Cornell's athletic buildings are fieldstone with limestone trim, this building is constructed of ground-face concrete block, white porcelain panels, and precast concrete. The varied colors and formal articulation of the different elements form a large-scale composition that can also be read as a subtractive graphic in dialogue with the surrounding stone buildings. Unlike the traditional campus model, this architecture clearly articulates the interior volumes that define the spatial and organizational hierarchy.

plans, from bottom: basement, ground level, second level

lobby and public stairs

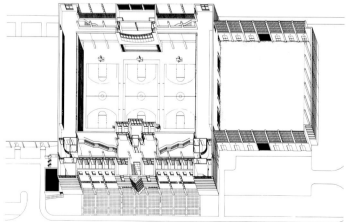

top: Fieldhouse with integrated climbing wall, bottom: axonometric of Fieldhouse and Basketball Arena

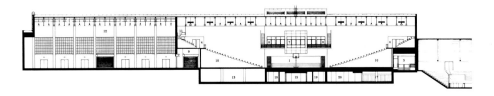

top: Basketball Arena with expanded seating,   bottom: section through Arena and Fieldhouse

competition basketball court showing coaches' offices and balcony

Ithaca, New York
1988–1990

This seven-story Theory Center occupies an imposing site that parallels Campus Road and borders the gorge at the southeast corner of the College of Engineering. The building defines a new threshold to the campus and establishes an architectural image for the College of Engineering.

The Theory Center is composed of a linear office building and an intersecting larger cylindrical laboratory building. The laboratory building responds to the College of Engineering's long-range master plan by providing over 100,000 square feet of flexible space to systematically accommodate varying laboratory needs within the college, while entire departments are temporarily relocated for existing building renovations.

The parti, generated from programmatic specifications—including natural light and operable windows in every faculty office—and site constraints, affords a formal juxtaposition between the curved office slab and eroded laboratory cylinder. The main entry articulates the intersection of the two primary forms, and marks the convergence of the two axes of Campus Road.

Theory Center at the College of Engineering, Cornell University

laboratory building from gorge

Glass-enclosed cylindrical stair towers at each end of the office slab recall the existing towers on campus and yield phenomenal views of the site topography as it drops to the lake. The towers are somewhat unnerving spaces, completely open vertical cages that provide a counterpoint to the more solid and enclosed massing of the office building.

A new graphic expression is established for the College of Engineering buildings, previously characterized by porcelain and glass curtain walls from the fifties. The office building is finished in alternating bands of gray brick and ribbon windows, and the more solid cylindrical laboratory building is reddish brown brick with punched square windows. The overall composition of elements appears at once engaged and disengaged. From the baseball field and stadium, one reads the full facade of the office building, but elsewhere on the campus, one reads and remembers the elements as overlaying or composite fragments of a collage.

intersection of office and laboratory buildings

top: view from Campus Road, bottom: aerial view from Barton Hall

top: interior of tower stairs, bottom: computer classroom

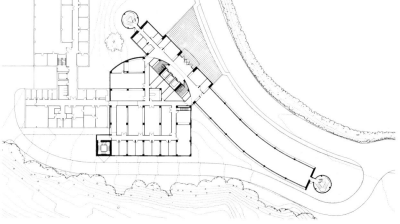

top: laboratory building and faculty office building from service drive, bottom: typical plan

corner detail showing tower stair, office building, and laboratory building

Bronx, New York
1985–1992

This multipurpose building for a community college in a Spanish-speaking area of the Bronx represents a composite program disposed within a dense urban context. The building program provides for classrooms, faculty and student offices, a swimming pool, gymnasium, and ancillary athletic spaces, a 1,200-seat proscenium theater, a repertory theater, faculty and student dining facilities, a campus store, an art gallery and studios, and a pedestrian bridge over the Grand Concourse, which connects to an existing library building.

Internally complex, the structure is restricted externally by its urban context. The Grand Concourse facade reinforces the built edge, creates a gateway to the college, and together with the original campus structure, defines an outdoor courtyard. The new tower and bridge serve as visual icons, establishing a sense of place and a new image for the campus in the community. The interior is organized around a five-story skylighted atrium, which acts as an interior cloister. Articulated horizontally with balconies and vertically with stairs, the atrium functions both as the major public space on the campus and the primary internal circulation volume.

Although site and budget constraints were severe, the program offered an opportunity to create architecture with significant presence, which will stimulate a sense of awareness and pride of place within the larger community.

Academic and Multipurpose Building, Eugenio Maria de Hostos Community College, The City University of New York

construction view from Grand Concourse

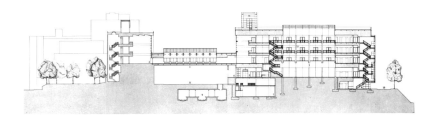

top right: bridge under construction, bottom: section through bridge and atrium

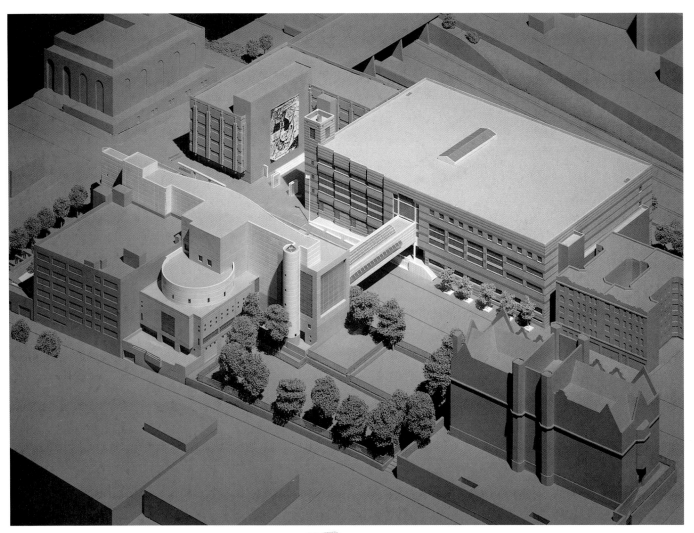

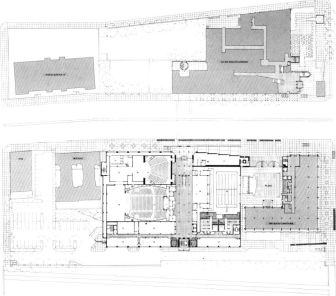

top: aerial view of model, bottom: Grand Concourse–level plan

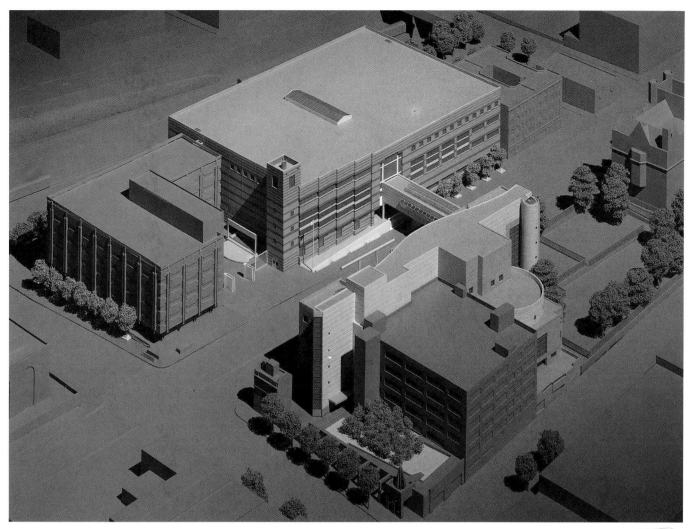

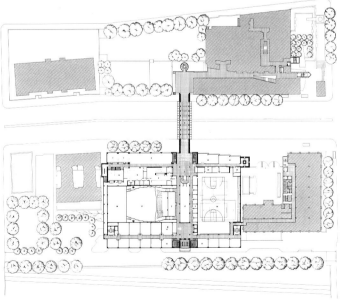

top: aerial view of model, bottom: pedestrian bridge–level plan

Amherst, New York
1985–1992

Theater Arts and Fine Arts Building,
State University of New York at Buffalo

partial view of south facade from vehicular entry circle, under construction

The master plan for this state university campus was realized over a ten-year period during the 1960s and 1970s. The location of the Theater Arts and Fine Arts Building on the last open site, coincidentally at the end of the primary cross-axis of the campus, redefines Coventry Circle as a major entry plaza for both athletic and performing-arts events.

The 264,000-square-foot building is asymmetrically bisected by a two-story skylighted atrium-gallery that defines the north-south axis and connects the two departments. The Fine Arts department consists of a student-faculty art gallery, sculpture, photography, and painting studios, and administrative and faculty offices. The Theater Arts department is larger, with an 1,800-seat proscenium theater, a 400-seat drama theater, two rehearsal theaters, a screening room, a media department and studio, dance studios, a full-service backstage area, and miscellaneous support spaces.

The art studios and performance spaces were designed to provide ideally flexible space for students and faculty. The combination of the two disciplines into a single building adds a programmatic and cultural dynamic to the center of the campus, increasing student and public access to the university's multidisciplinary activities.

To break down the scale and articulate the massing, horizontally banded brick in three colors and sizes is used as the primary exterior material, counterpointed by white porcelain panels that define the public volumes, circulation spaces, and stage houses. The resulting collage of forms, planes, and fragments reinforces the programmatic variation and architectural topology of the building.

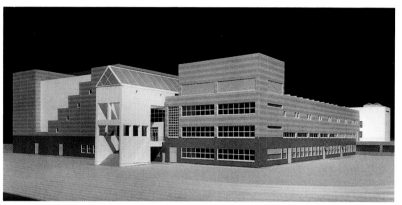

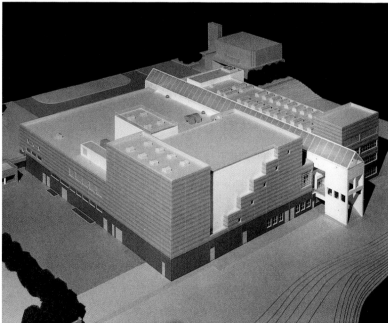

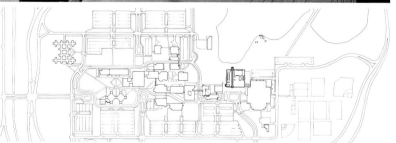

top: southwest view of model from lake, middle: southeast aerial view of model, bottom: site plan

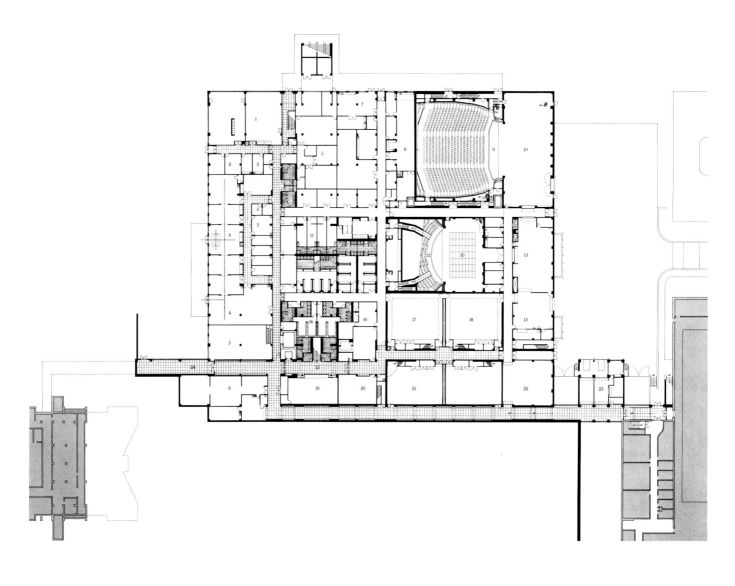

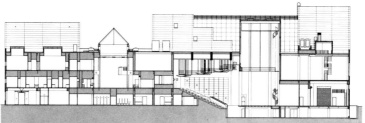

top: lower-level plan, bottom: section through gallery and performance theater

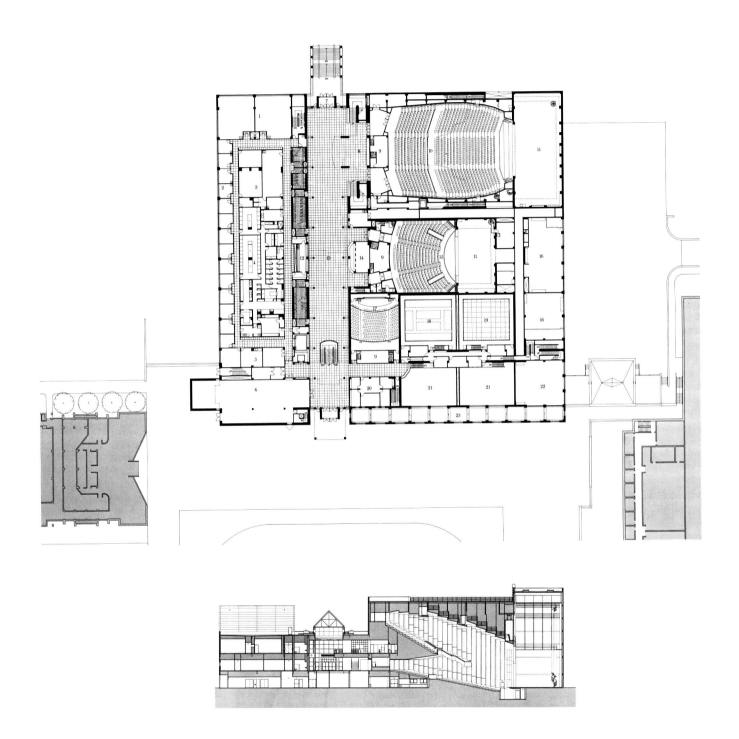

top: ground-level plan, bottom: section through proscenium theater and arts studios

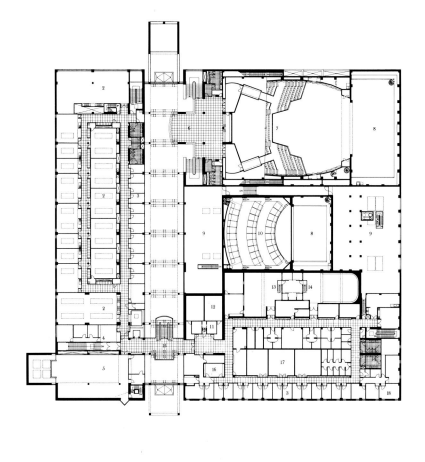

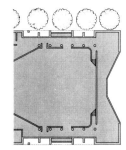

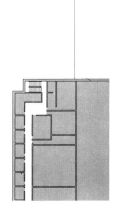

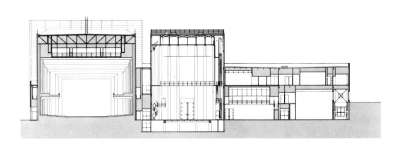

top: second-level plan, bottom: section through proscenium theater, performance theater, black-box theater, and dance studios

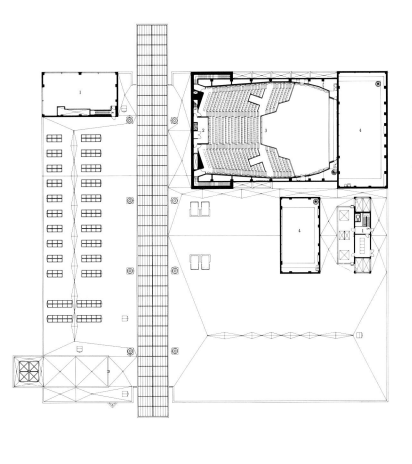

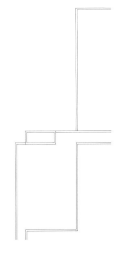

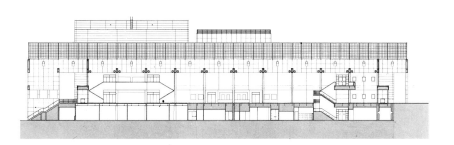

top: third-level plan, bottom: section through exhibition gallery

Charlotte, North Carolina
1986–1989

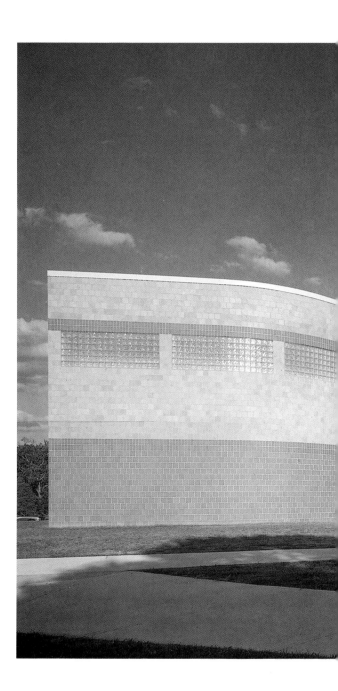

Sited in a former parking lot, the College of Architecture is the first building to be constructed on the perimeter of this campus designed in the 1960s. Like many other campuses, it lacked a sense of place, and its outdoor spaces were either residual or undefined. Establishing an alternative master plan for the next edge, or architectural layer, was integral to the program. In siting the new building, we set a precedent for the design of outdoor spaces between buildings and initiated a new parking strategy to resolve the random campus circulation system, using perimeter garages as transfer nodes or gateways into the campus.

The College of Architecture had a strongly defined program, and a clear pedagogical position that called for all the physical laboratories—welding, mechanics, structures—to be integrated with the architecture studio system. Interaction between faculty and students was crucial, and the building had to accommodate a flexible program.

Organized around a linear, two-story, skylighted circulation and exhibition courtyard, the 83,000-square-foot structure is defined at the entry by an open stair and elevator tower and at the student lounge-lecture theater end by a grandstand stair. The courtyard entry terminates a major campus circulation axis and provides access to a multiuse exhibition gallery, a 200-seat lecture theater, and administrative offices. Seminar rooms and faculty offices flank the exhibition court, and parallel studios and shops line the adjacent facades.

The building's aesthetic and physical accessibility encourages the mandate of a learning and teaching laboratory for the study of architecture. It is intended to foster criticism and exploration as an essential part of the discovery process.

College of Architecture, University of North Carolina

89

top: partial west facade and entry courtyard, bottom left: northwest corner, bottom right: southwest facade from pedestrian walk

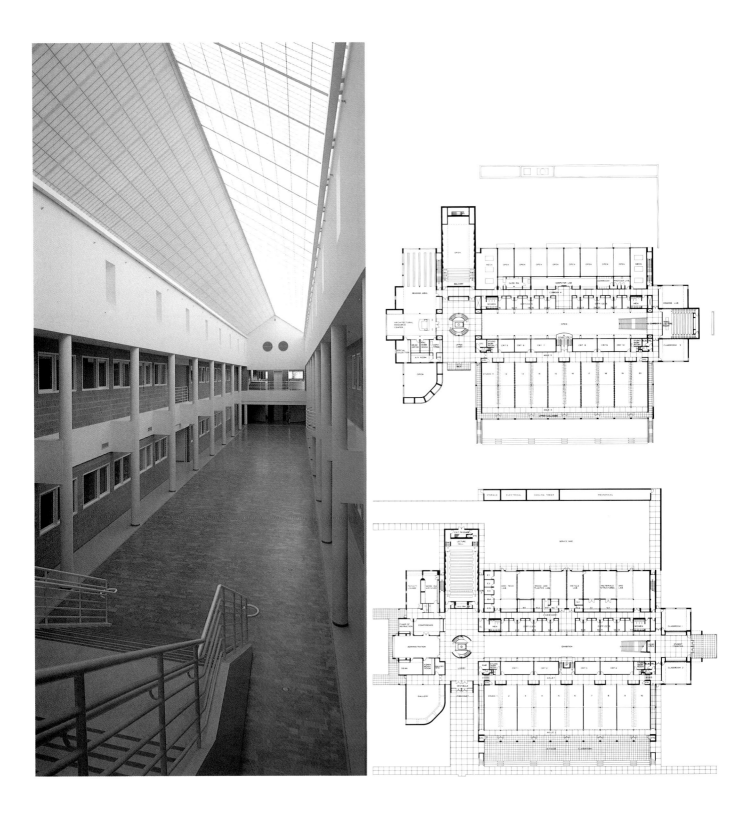

left: exhibition hall, right: ground-level plan and second-level plan

top left: lecture theater, top right: second-level architecture studios, bottom: exhibition gallery

detail of elevator and public stair from second level

detail of elevator and public stair from entrance hall

Oberlin, Ohio
1988–1991

North Campus Dining Building, Oberlin College

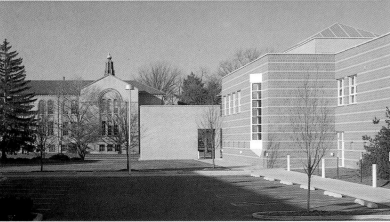

To reinforce the intimate scale of the Oberlin campus, the building was organized to support the residential-house model of the college. The site is adjacent to both institutional buildings and typical Oberlin houses, which are three-story structures with front porches. The massing of the North Campus Dining Building reconciles the divergent scales by reinterpreting the porch-house prototype into an institutional model.

Articulated by three identical, pyramidal skylighted dining halls, or houses, on the second level, the 48,000-square-foot building serves 800 students and faculty. A continuous linear element unites the three volumes, providing outdoor dining terraces on the upper level and a street-front porch on the lower level. An entry plaza offers access to the three house entries, lounges, and administrative offices. The inverted organization provides natural light from above in a typically gray climate zone, and allows three separate dining halls with common service and kitchen to be organized in one structure.

The exterior material palette consists of two colors of horizontally banded brick and cast stone that relate to nearby buildings by Cass Gilbert. By reversing Gilbert's palette, which is primarily limestone with brick trim, the dining hall makes abstract contextual references while hierarchically articulating its volumetric forms.

top: west facade from campus, bottom: pedestrian walk showing Cass Gilbert science building in background

pedestrian walk with entry porch and terrace above

corner of south facade

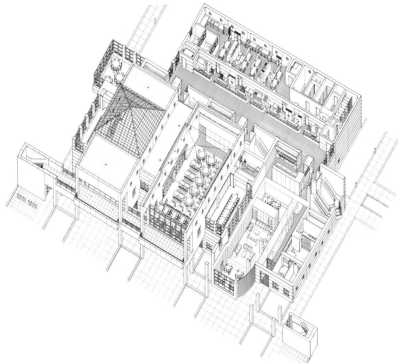

top: typical main dining space, bottom: axonometric view showing ground, second, and roof levels

servery with dining hall beyond

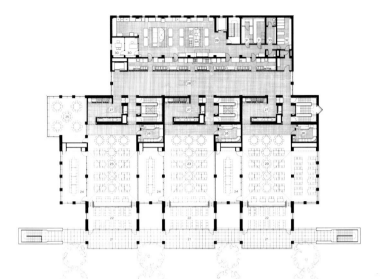

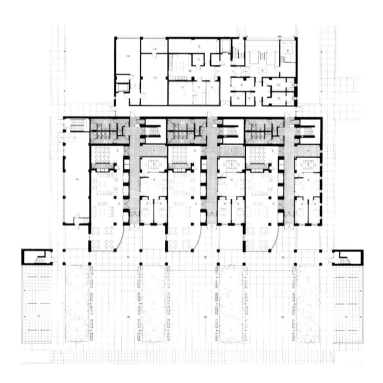

left top: typical student lounge space, left bottom: south interior stair, right: ground-level plan and second-level plan

typical dining hall

Durham, North Carolina
1988–1994

Center for Jewish Life, Duke University

aerial view of model from College Road

This building will house the Hillel Center for Duke University, and will also serve as the religious and celebratory center of Jewish life in Durham. Our primary concern was to establish a sense of place for the activities the program encompassed.

The building is approached from Campus Drive by a bridge that crosses over the heavily wooded, sloping site and arrives at an entry courtyard. Located on the roof of the building, the courtyard recalls one of the classic strategies of modernism by replacing the ground with the roof as the major outdoor space. Modulating the roof court are the volumetric extensions of the primary elements of the program.

A major stair and two-story gallery link the roof entry to the ground-floor entry below. Lighted by a glass-block zone on the roof that marks the bridge extension, the gallery provides entrance to a dining hall, multipurpose room, and sanctuary on the ground level, and a library, administrative offices, lounge, and sanctuary balcony on the second level. The balcony allows the sanctuary to hold both Orthodox and Conservative services.

The masonry building is an assemblage of objects made complex and articulate by the simultaneous manipulation of plan and section.

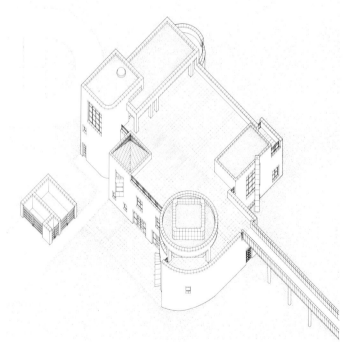

top: site plan, bottom: axonometric

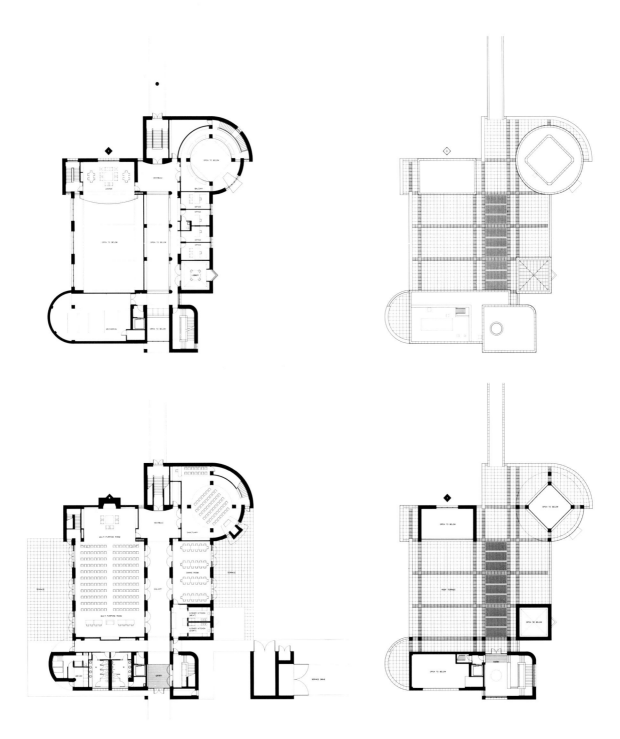

plans, from bottom left to top right: ground level, second level, roof terrace, roof

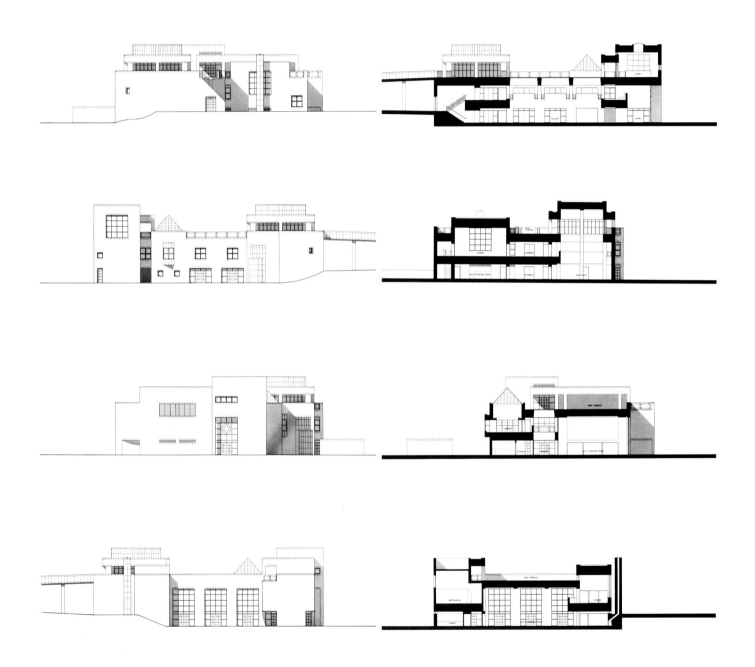

Cambridge, Massachusetts
1989–1991

The design of a new home for the Busch Reisinger Museum proved to be theoretically and technically challenging. While the new building is connected to a traditional structure, the Fogg Museum, it is also adjacent to Le Corbusier's modern masterpiece, the Carpenter Center. Werner Otto Hall bridges this dual context as an infill facade in the existing streetscape and as a critical site element in the larger urban plan.

The program required new permanent exhibition galleries for the Busch Reisinger collection, a changing exhibition gallery, study archives, administrative offices, and a fine-arts library. It was also necessary to respond to constraints imposed by building above an underground library-stack structure with limited load-bearing capacity and aligning the new structure with the floor levels of the Fogg Museum.

Werner Otto Hall, Harvard University

left: intersection with Fogg Museum, right: view from Quincy Street between Fogg Museum and Carpenter Center

east entry facade from street level

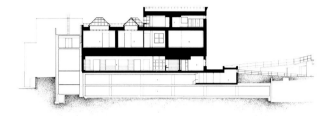

Quincy Street

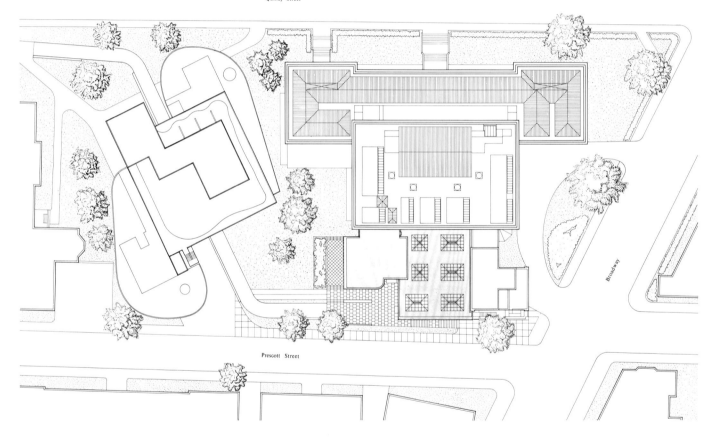

Prescott Street

Broadway

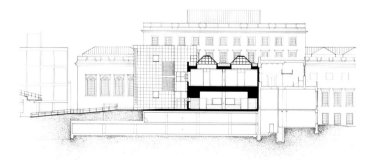

top: section looking toward Prescott Street, middle: site plan, bottom: section-elevation from Prescott Street

The solution refers to the formal organization of the Fogg Museum design. One side of the peripheral circulation of the existing museum's courtyard extends into the new building, connecting the two major massing elements of the design. To the north are the primary spaces: the library reading room on the ground floor and the permanent-collection galleries on the second floor. The two-story volume extends the central axis of the Fogg to Prescott Street, where the new building presents its primary facade. To the south are support and smaller-scale spaces: the library-staff offices on the ground floor, the temporary exhibition gallery on the second floor, and the study archives on the third floor. These spaces are organized in a three-story element, set back from the street and rotated to address the Carpenter Center. The interlocked massing of the two elements reinforces the street plane and completes the orthogonal building framework that defines the Carpenter Center site.

Le Corbusier's compelling site-circulation idea is also resolved. The Carpenter Center ramp, which was intended to provide a public mid-block walkway through the building from Quincy Street to Prescott Street, ended in the Fogg's rear yard without a connection to the sidewalk. The design extends the path of the ramp onto a new plaza from which one can either enter the library or descend a new exterior stair to the street.

Limestone, pewter-gray porcelain metal panels, and flame-finished green granite constitute the exterior materials. The color and texture palettes establish an independent graphic image for the building and relate to both the monolithic concrete of the Carpenter Center and the brick and limestone of the Fogg Museum.

The building design uses abstraction, reinterpretation, and inversion of traditional readings to address the context and reinforce the literal and historical sense of collage on the site, in the belief that architectural history should be understood in terms of pervasive principles rather than style. History is viewed as a continuous dialogue between old and new that is more profoundly enriched by interpretation than imitation.

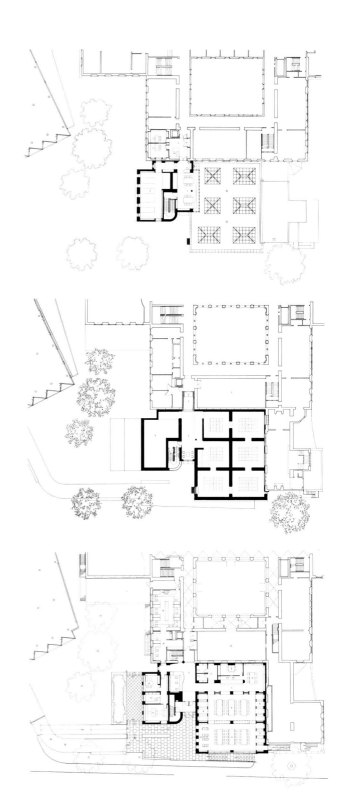

plans, from bottom: ground level, second level, third level

Fogg Museum and south facade of addition from Carpenter Center ramp

overall view, showing completion-extension of Carpenter Center ramp through site

south facade from Carpenter Center

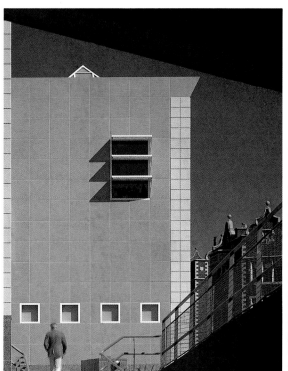

top left: detail of south facade, top right: south louvered window from gallery, bottom: main reading room of fine-arts library

entry-introduction gallery to Busch Reisinger Museum

entry-introduction gallery to Busch Reisinger Museum

permanent-collection galleries

detail of stair

top: pyramidal skylights on gallery roof outside study archives, bottom: study archives

east facade from corner of Prescott Street and Broadway

earlier work, from top: 1976 Thomas & Betts Corporation Building; 1978 Knoll International Building;
1979 Triangle Pacific Corporation Building; 1980 First City Bank Building

Corporate Buildings and Projects

Long Island City, New York
1983–1988

International Design Center I & II

top: bridge from Center II to Center I, bottom: Centers II and I from parking plaza

The International Design Center is a complex of four typical reinforced-concrete loft buildings of World War I vintage. The first phase of the project, now complete, was the renovation of buildings I and II into design centers for the furniture and textile industries.

Center II was a seven-story building with an open courtyard. A trussed bridge at the open end of the plan provided the opportunity to create two major spaces: a skylighted interior atrium and an open entry court with an elevator core and lobby. A new catwalk beam for exterior lighting and display unifies the entry facade and acts as a gateway to the complex.

A decorative stair was added at the north end of the Center II atrium. Four new steel bridges span the atrium at the fourth-floor level, vertically articulating the space and forming an implied second ceiling. A translucent, paneled skylight transforms the once-open courtyard into a public room that orients the continuous open-balcony galleries adjoining the showroom spaces on each floor.

Center I, completed after Center II, is a horizontal five-story building organized along the same principles. The courtyard was enclosed to create a central atrium surrounded by showrooms. A cascading double stair was added to one side of the space, connecting all balcony levels with a central exposed elevator bank. The Center I building is entered from a recessed arcade facing the Center II parking plaza, or from a ramped connecting bridge at levels three, four, and five. Spanning the street with its red metal and oculus fenestration, the eighty-foot bridge is the project's graphic symbol.

Center II lobby with new elevator tower

Center II atrium

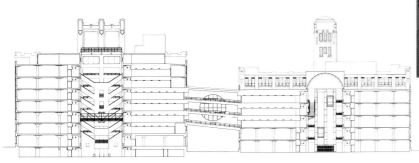

top left: Center II atrium, bottom left: section through Centers II and I, right, top to bottom: typical elevator-lobby balcony, main stair, and elevator balcony bridge in Center II

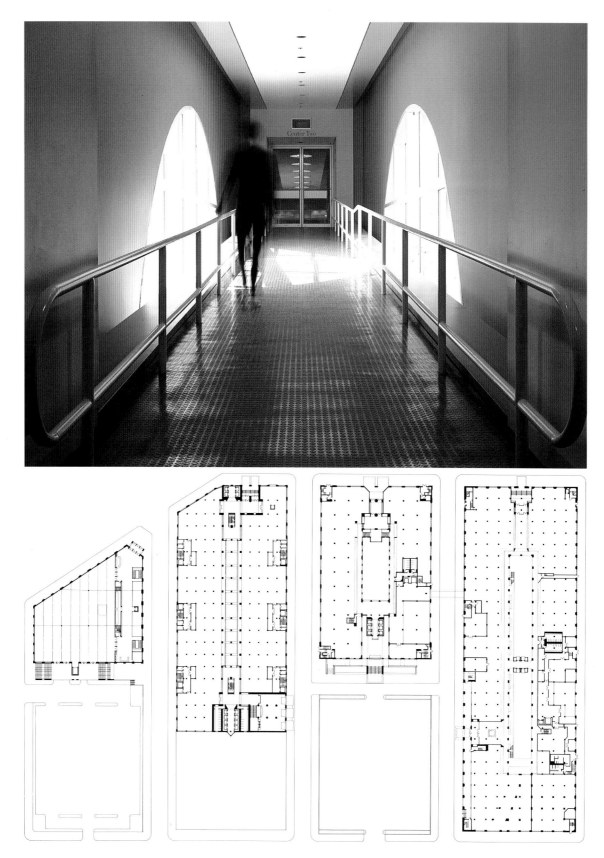

top: ramp connection in bridge between Centers II and I, bottom right to left: plans of Centers IV, III, II, and I

Center I atrium

New York, New York
1985–1991

This fifty-two-story office building occupies the west block-front of Broadway between Forty-seventh and Forty-eighth streets. The massing of the building and the articulation of the details reflect the aspirations of a traditional skyscraper to present an appropriately scaled public building at the pedestrian base and a strong silhouette on the skyline.

The building forms address the diagonal of Broadway as well as the orthogonal Manhattan street grid. The stepped base responds to the diagonal, relating to the pedestrian scale of the street and the fabric of six- and seven-story buildings in the Times Square area. The segmented curve of the double-height mechanical floor forms the transition from the rotated base to the orthogonal tower. The building culminates in a highly articulated top, presenting varied silhouettes from different distances and angles within the city.

Creating a layered graphic of blue-green glass, white patterned glass, mirrored glass, silver-gray aluminum panels, and polished stainless steel, the curtain wall encourages multiple facade readings. The changing quality of natural light on the building produces images of both opacity and reflectivity, creating a simultaneous sense of fluidity and permanence.

Running the length of the building from Forty-seventh to Forty-eighth streets, the entrance lobby is a grand formal space rendered in marble, granite, and wood that contrasts with the glass and metal of the exterior. A geometric floor pattern of white, black, and green marble and a coffered wood ceiling create a dense, articulated public space.

Solomon Equities, Inc.

top: detail at top of tower, bottom: detail at base of tower

view from New Jersey looking east across Hudson River

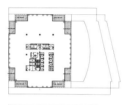

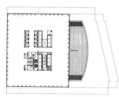

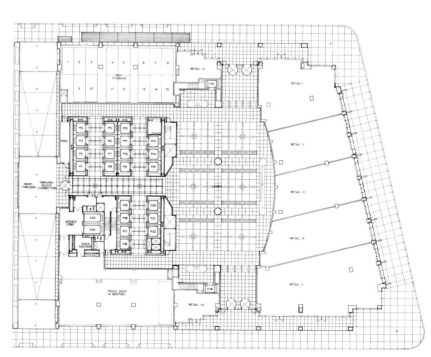

top left: mid-block pedestrian passage and automobile drop-off, top right: view from southwest, bottom: ground-level plan and typical upper-level plans

east facade from Broadway

skylighted arcade between main lobby and automobile drop-off

top: main lobby, bottom left: typical elevator lobby, bottom right: typical elevator interior

Greensboro, North Carolina
1985–1987

Located adjacent to a main Greensboro highway, this 150,000-square-foot office building and distribution center is the first of three phases of a 450,000-square-foot project. The building is planned to accommodate the company's future expansion needs to the east and west.

To provide maximum flexibility in the floor plates, the elevator and stair cores are located in the entrance tower on the south facade. The structure is reinforced concrete, cantilevered from interior columns to the perimeter. On the south facade the concrete floor planes extend to act as integrated sunscreens, adding depth to the recessed glass curtain wall. On the north facade the glass is set flush with the concrete floor edge, creating a contrapuntal facade reading. Three types of glass denote floor, sill, and suspended ceiling datums.

In contrast to the exposed concrete frame, the entrance tower is clad in white tile, glass block, white metal panels, and glass. The five-story, balconied tower reads as an object against a frame, and defines the entry plaza and the landscape between the building and parking area. On the tower's solid face, square punched windows at each floor level align with the circular windows of the elevator cabs, recalling the circulation sequence. Built with basic construction technology, this generic building type is transformed by innovative planning and the exploration of compositional alternatives.

IBM Greensboro

intersection of south facade with elevator core

top left: detail of elevator-core facade,   bottom left: porthole view from elevator stops,   top right: entry plaza to lobby,   bottom right: model showing proposed three phases

top: view from typical elevator bridge through lobby, bottom: ground-level plan

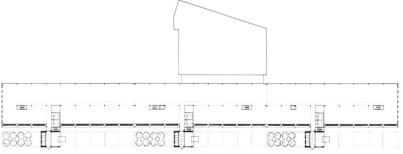

top left: view of typical elevator bridge, top right: view of lobby, bottom: typical floor plan

Lake Buena Vista, Florida
1989–1991

Disney World's new 145,000-square-foot Convention Center is an addition to Walt Disney's visionary Contemporary Hotel, completed in 1971. A new two-and-a-half-acre entry plaza joins the two buildings and leads to a new porte-cochere entry for the Hotel. The addition contains a 45,000-square-foot main ballroom that holds 3,300 persons and can be divided into three multipurpose spaces, a 7,000-square-foot ballroom, three prefunction spaces, five meeting rooms, and a full-service kitchen with loading facilities.

The Convention Center's horizontal silhouette, reinforced by a strong color palette, contrasts with the vertical, gridded facade of the Hotel. Four major forms create the collage-assemblage: the curved, striped primary volume of the main ballroom and prefunction gallery; the entry canopy, a skylighted outdoor porte-cochere for cars and buses; and the two rotundas, one connecting to the Hotel with stairs, escalators, and a glass-block bridge, and the other accented by a square-punched window, which presents an iconic form on the more visible west corner.

The sequence of interior spaces, which culminates in the main ballroom, heightens the memory of these forms. Defined by a triangulated, polished aluminum grid, the ballroom ceiling is an illusive, reflective multiprism that appears to float over the space, restating the object-frame theme of the parti.

Contemporary Resort Convention Center, Walt Disney World

top: entry plaza and vehicular entry arcade, bottom: overall view from Lake Buena Vista

top: vehicular entry arcade

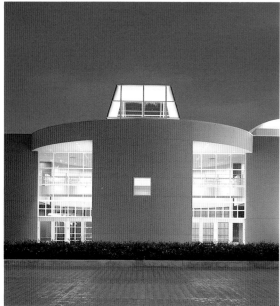

top: south rotunda from Hotel, bottom: south rotunda from plaza

141

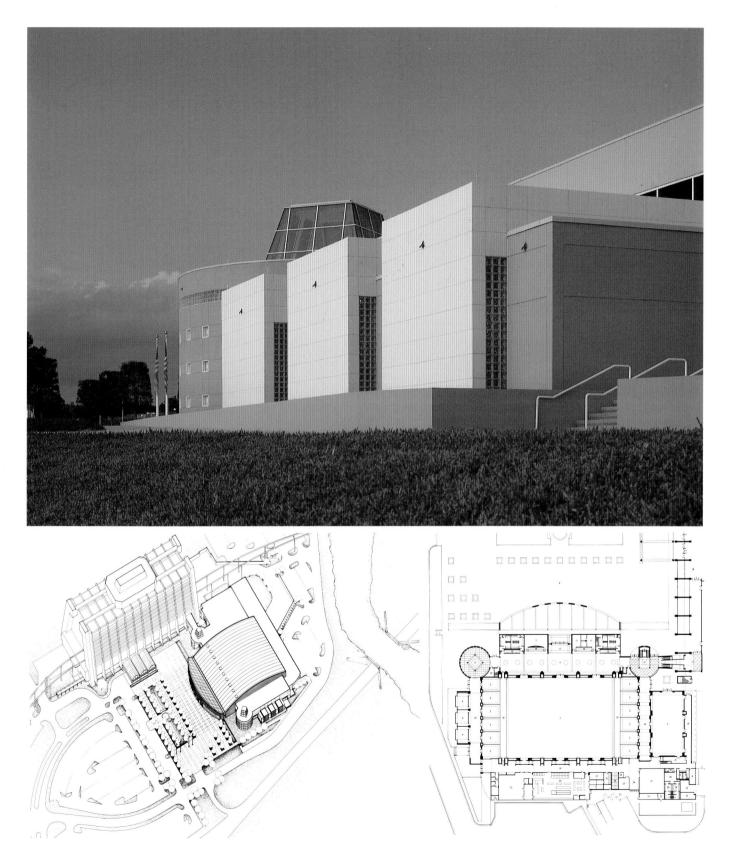

top: north facade, bottom left: axonometric, bottom right: ground-level plan

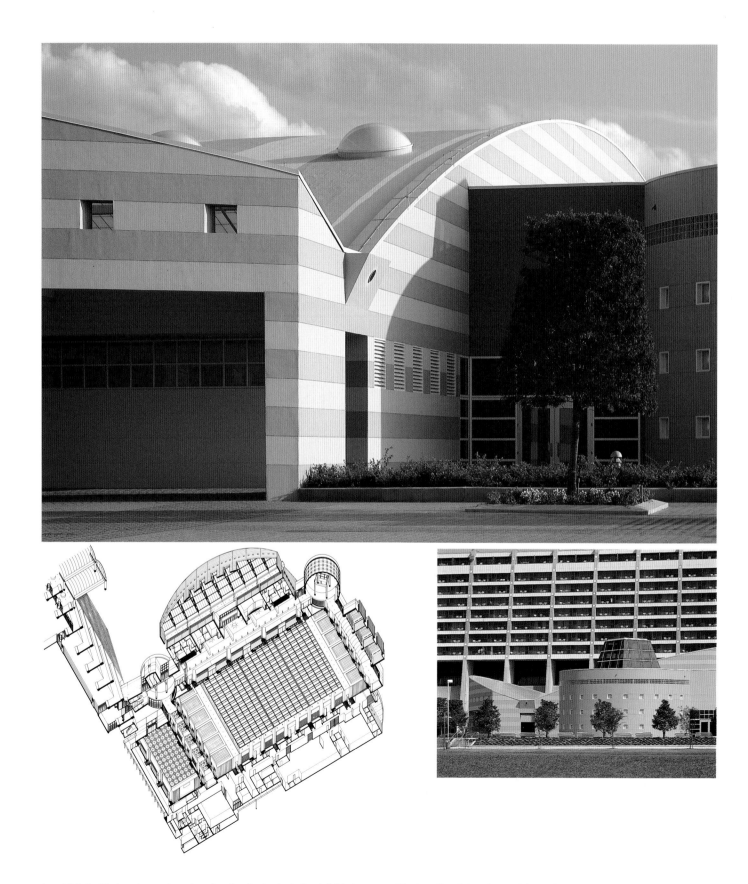

top: detail of vehicular entry arcade, main roof, and north rotunda, bottom left: interior axonometric viewed from below, bottom right: north rotunda

interior of north rotunda

top left: south rotunda from courtyard, top right: bridge from Hotel to south rotunda, bottom: overall view of south rotunda showing escalators and bridge connection to Hotel

main prefunction space

top: prefunction space to north rotunda, bottom: typical meeting room

main ballroom

Lake Buena Vista, Florida
1990–1992

Bonnet Creek Golf Clubhouse, Walt Disney World

northeast facade from lake

Unlike most recent Disney architecture, our buildings at Walt Disney World do not conform to the notion of theming. The "theme" of the Bonnet Creek Golf Clubhouse, as well as that of the Contemporary Resort Convention Center, is the architecture itself—the memory of forms and space, reinforced by color and graphics, establishing a primary sense of presence.

Sited on the knoll of a golf course overlooking a lake, the Clubhouse building is an object with a composite identity. Its silhouette, visible from a distance across the greens, is experienced more immediately through the vehicular arrival sequence. The integrated use of color intensifies the multiple images and forms of a simple internal program: a golf shop, bar and grill, banquet-multipurpose room, kitchen, lockers, administrative offices, maintenance facilities, golf-cart storage, and staff facilities. The goal was to transform the traditional golf-clubhouse image into a site-responsive, architecturally defined object-collage in the landscape.

top: southwest facade from entry road, bottom: stair connecting arcade to golf-cart pickup

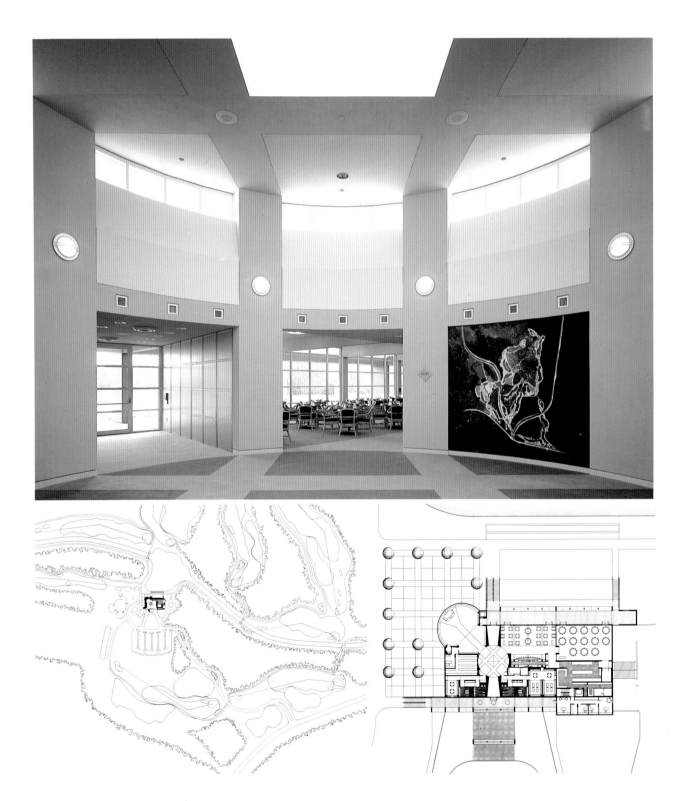

top: entry rotunda, bottom left: site plan, bottom right: main-level plan

top: multiuse space, bottom: covered terrace overlooking lake

Beverly Hills, California
1990–1994

The David Geffen Company

aerial view of model from southeast

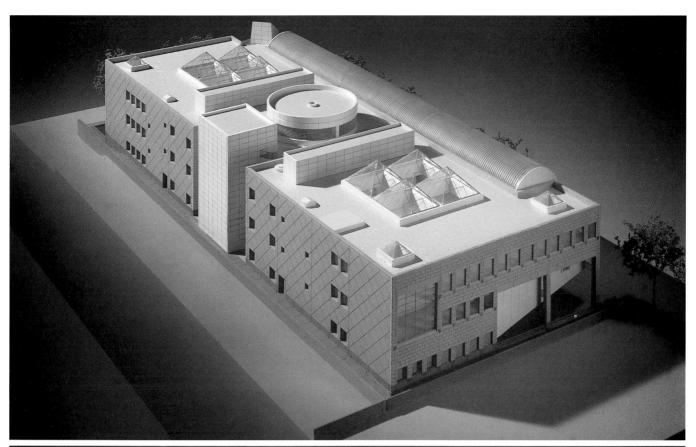

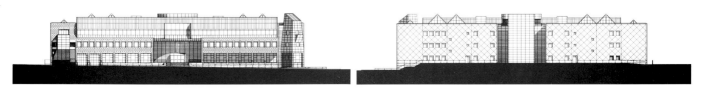

top: aerial view of model from northwest, middle: view of model from Third Street, bottom: south elevation and north elevation

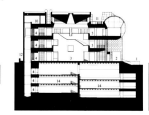
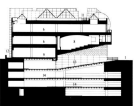

top: entry circulation rotunda, bottom: east elevation, west elevation, section through rotunda, section through theater

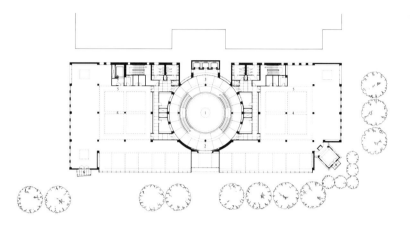

The David Geffen Company building is a 90,000-square-foot corporate headquarters located in the Beverly Hills industrial district, where zoning restrictions limit the height of buildings to three stories. The typical cornice line along the street is reinterpreted by a barrel-vaulted, Kal-wall roof running the length of the building and incorporating the third-floor offices.

Site and program variants are exploited to create a complex, hierarchically asymmetrical building. The theater marks the garage entry and ramp; the main conference rooms occupy a tower at the corner, adjoining a plaza and reflecting pool; and the main entry circulation space projects from the long facade as a cylindrical gallery-rotunda. The four-story limestone rotunda with exposed stairs, curving balconies, elevator core, reversed-cone ceiling, and clerestory windows is the central volume in the composition.

Related more to residential work than to earlier corporate projects, the building is elaborate and complex in its sectional manipulations. The Euro-Disney Convention Center, designed at the same time, was informed by this exploration. Though not a large building, the project is developmentally significant. The ideological and literal structure addresses issues of collage, assemblage, materiality, carved space, and frame-object relationships, achieving a point of distillation and unity.

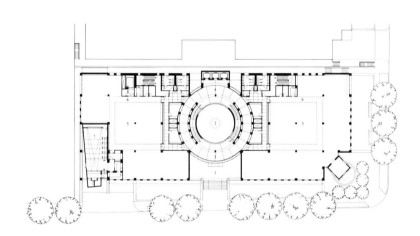

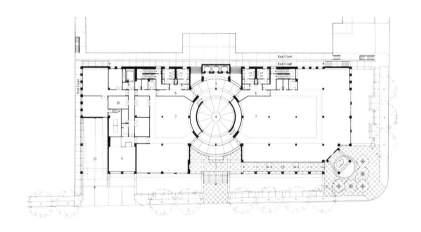

plans, from bottom: ground level, second level, third level

Frankfurt am Main, Germany
1991–1994

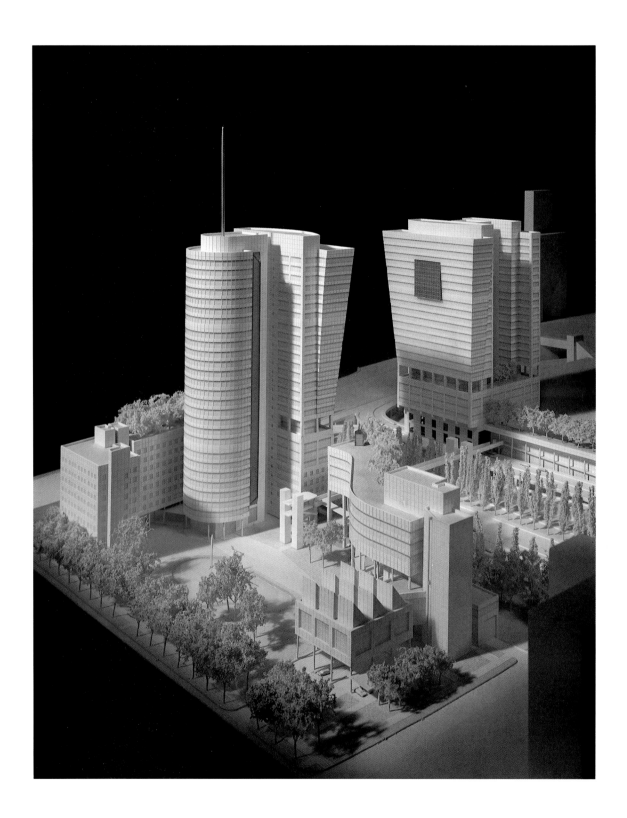

Stadtportalhäuser

aerial view of model from north showing museum park, Bosch Corporation building, two speculative office buildings, and hotel

This gateway project is located at the intersection of a major boulevard into the city of Frankfurt and the edge of a large international exposition center. The design produced a compelling plan graphic and massing collage of varying scales and multiple images. The complexity and volumetric configurations were specific responses to the site and program, which includes a museum and office building for the Bosch Corporation, two speculative office buildings, and a hotel. The design resolution was influenced both by the importance of maintaining the site trees and an open park space and by the presence of an existing railroad bridge, road system, and exposition structures.

The silhouettes viewed from a distance and the memories elicited by the architecture as a whole are reinforced by the more immediate experiences at grade and the complexities of land and building intersections. Essential to the project's composition and image are the two similar wedge-shaped office buildings whose facades define the gate and the dissimilar masses that extend from these facades to either side of the boulevard.

As the first European competition for our office, the scale and complexity of the architectural and urban resolutions represent a learning and research experience. The issues and strategies explored are an excellent resource for future investigations.

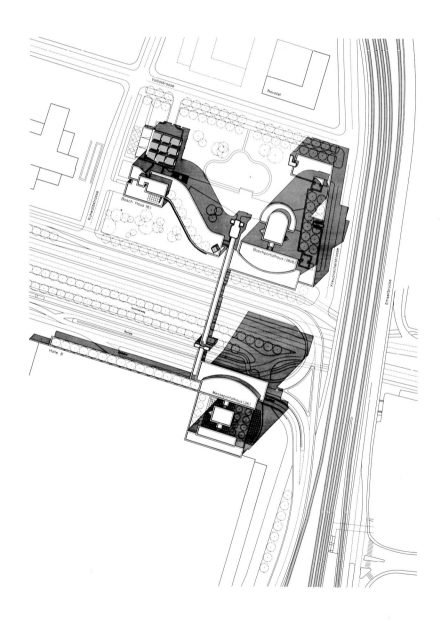

site plan

aerial view of model from south

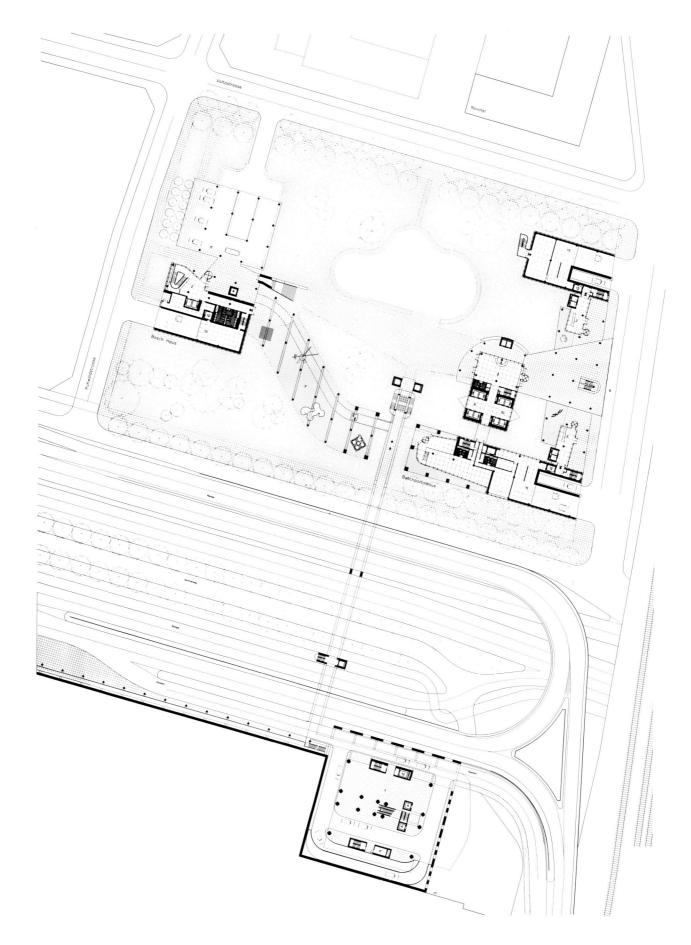

overall ground-level plan

top: aerial view of model from east, bottom: ground-level view from east

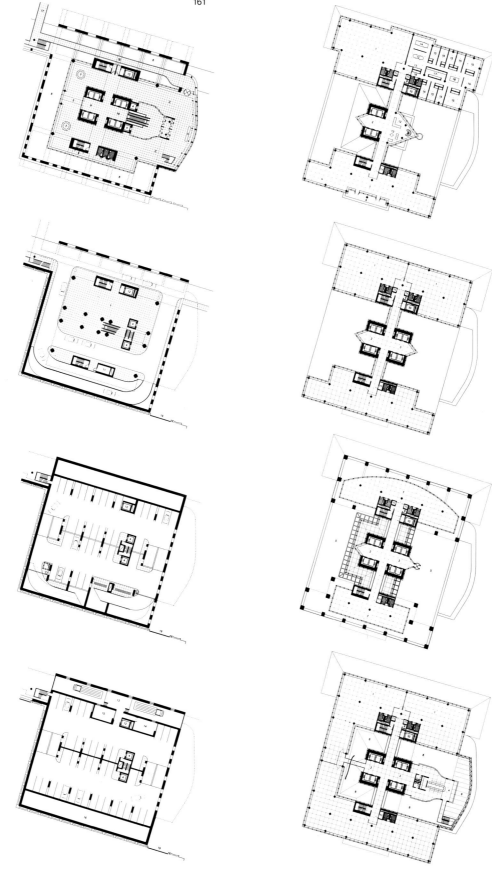

plans of speculative office building on south site, bottom left to top right: garage levels, vehicular entry level, lobby level, mezzanine level, terrace level, typical office levels

aerial view of model from north

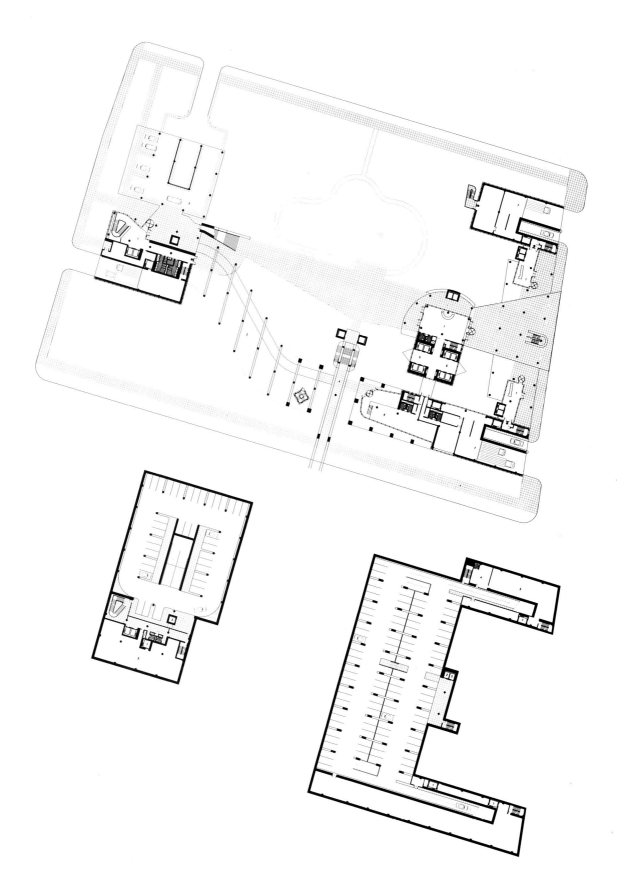

garage plans and ground-level plan of north-site office building, museum, and hotel

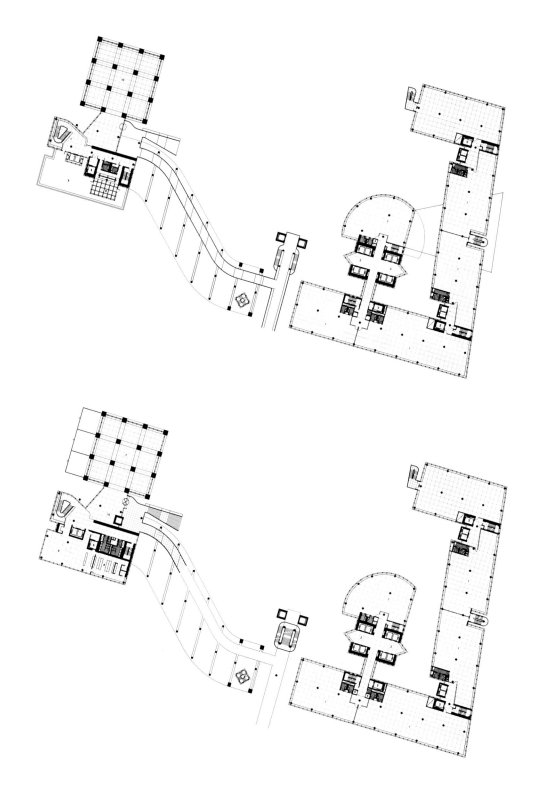

second-level and third-level plans of north-site office building, museum, and hotel

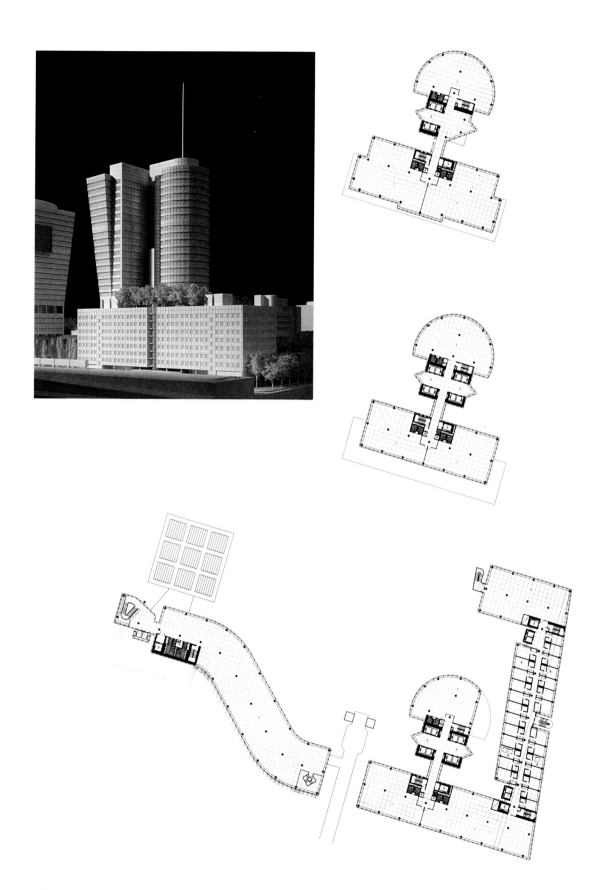

left: view of model from northwest, right: fourth-level plan of north-site office building, museum, and hotel and typical upper-level plans of north-site office building

Marne-la-Vallée, France
1992–

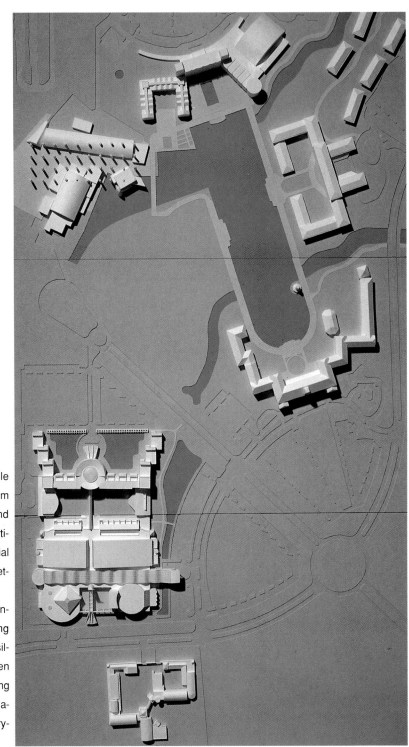

The Convention Center and Hotel is the largest single building project to date at Euro-Disney. The 750-room Convention Hotel with restaurants, meeting facilities, and health spa has direct access to a 300,000-square-foot multidimensional Convention Center with a 2,000-seat industrial theater, exhibition pavilion, ballrooms, lecture theater, meeting rooms, and full food-service facilities.

Located at the entrance to the complex, the building consciously rejects the decorated-box theme of the existing hotels and is perceived instead as a collection of forms, silhouettes, and facades expressing the relationship between exterior form and interior volume. The sequential ordering and integration of exterior spaces, transitions, and circulation organizes the interior and articulates a constantly varying silhouette and massing.

Convention Center and Hotel, Euro-Disney

site model

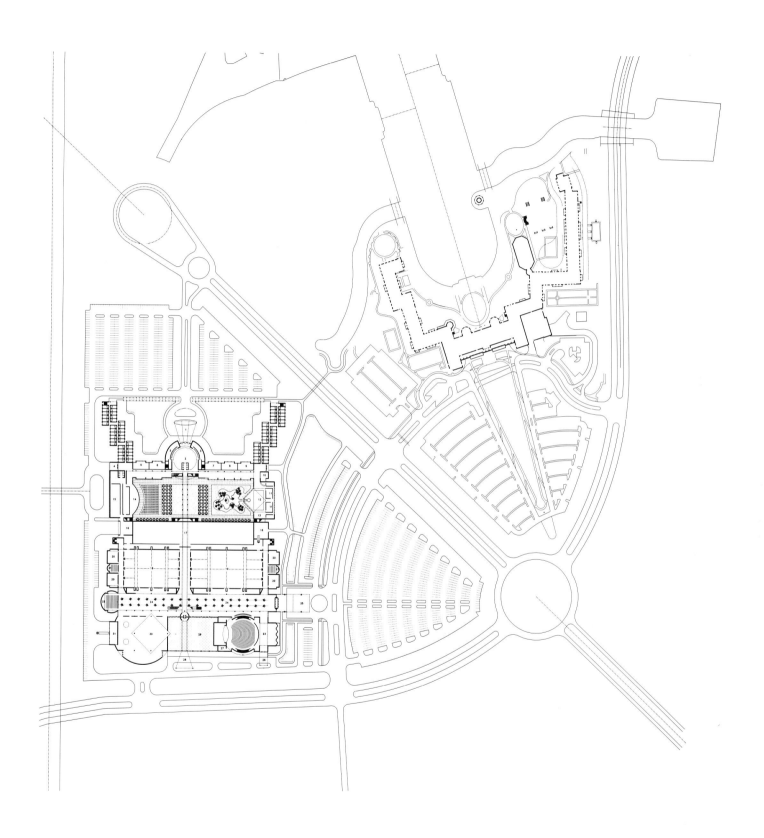

ground-level and site plan

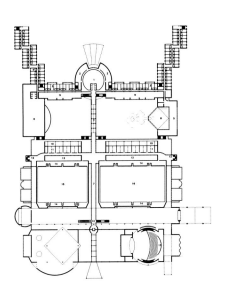 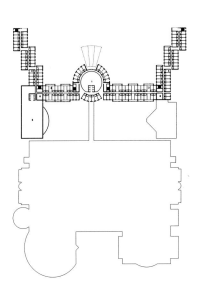 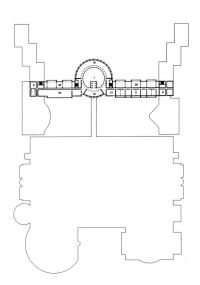

top: aerial view of model from park, bottom: second-level plan, typical upper-level plan, and roof plan of Hotel

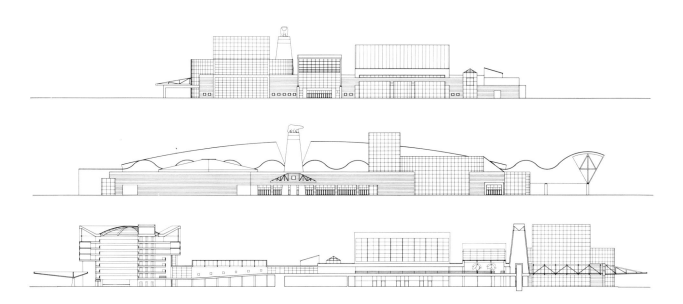

top: aerial view of model from access road, bottom: section, elevation from access road, elevation from park road

Marne-la-Vallée, France
1991–1992

Euro-Disney's Golf Clubhouse is initially seen as an object on the horizon. Three distinct roof forms—a dome, a barrel vault, and a curved, segmented shed—distinguish the primary programmatic volumes in contrast to the natural setting.

Connecting the separate site and building circulation systems, the vehicular entry porch with a skylighted canopy extends through the building as the public access gallery. The 11,000-square-foot ground floor houses locker rooms, a store, a restaurant-bar and kitchen, and administrative offices. Two large exterior terraces provide ground-floor views to the golf course. The 9,500-square-foot lower level accommodates parking and service for 120 golf carts, staff support space, and a vehicular ramp from grade.

As in all of our work for Walt Disney World and Euro-Disney, the Golf Clubhouse is an abstract collage of form and color. It is intended to evoke memories and expectations, as opposed to making literal or figural allusions.

Golf Clubhouse, Euro-Disney

left: entry canopy, right: entry facade from drive

bottom: entry gallery

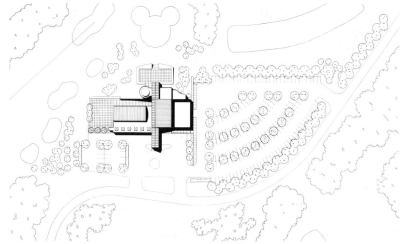

top: Clubhouse from putting green, bottom: site plan

top: Clubhouse from golf-cart plaza, bottom: golf store

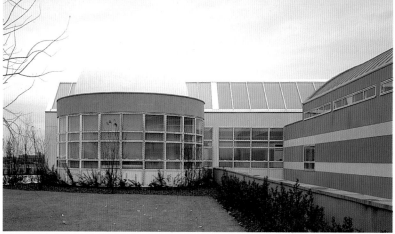

top: Clubhouse from green, bottom: Clubhouse snack bar

bottom: interior of Clubhouse snack bar

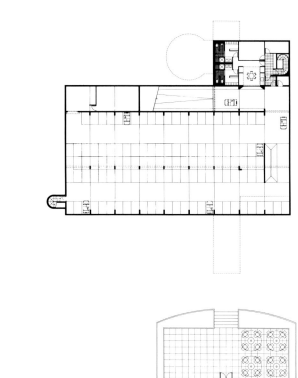

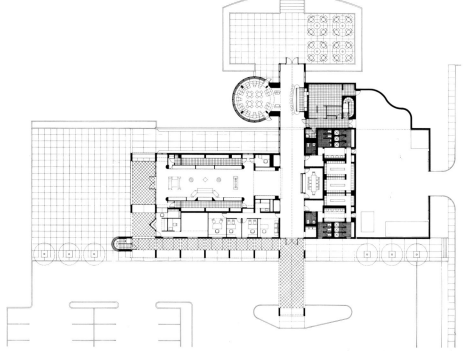

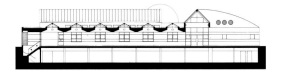

section through arcade, main-level plan, lower-level plan

arcade

earlier work, from top: 1973 Pearl's Restaurant; 1976 Swirl, Inc., Showrooms;
1977 Evans Partnership Offices; 1979 Reliance Group Holdings, Inc., Offices

Building Interiors

Chicago, Illinois
1984–1985

Knoll International Showroom

entry from public gallery

Our philosophy in designing showrooms has been to create a gallery or museumlike space for changing displays, rather than singular, topical environments. The Knoll International Showroom is flexible enough to adapt to various spatial interventions, and yet the architecture maintains a sense of density and clarity.

The project's planning grid was derived from the dimensional modules of an existing lightwell, centrally located in the 18,000-square-foot space, and two existing rows of columns. The lightwell was transformed from a transparent void at the center of the space into a solid volume of white glass, providing a fixed object against which the continually changing products are displayed.

Defined spaces line the perimeter, leaving an open plan between its gridded glass wall and the white glass center object. A suspended ceiling grid of painted wood allows for multiple lighting sources and hangings, while maintaining a unified visual plane over the entire space.

top: showroom from entry, bottom: detail of typical interior panel wall

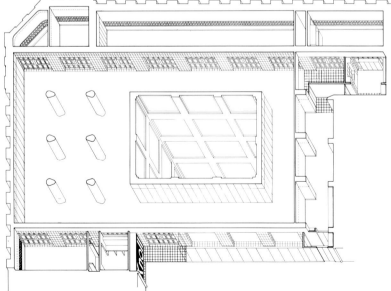

top: showroom-exhibition space, bottom: axonometric

top and bottom: views of showroom

Chicago, Illinois
1985–1986

Lexecon, Inc.

elevator lobby and reception-waiting area

Lexecon, Inc., offers the combined expertise of lawyers, economists, and legal scholars to corporate clients contemplating mergers and acquisitions. The environment was designed to project a sense of permanence and solidity appropriate to a consulting firm with Fortune 500 clients, and to support the organization's interdisciplinary, collegial culture.

An entry gallery, defined by parallel rows of existing large columns, initiates the sequence to the transition-reception-secretarial spaces at each end, which then access the perimeter offices. The wide circulation corridors support Louis Kahn's notion that the incidental meeting of peers is where the most important and unedited discussions occur. The corridors also serve as viewing galleries for the senior partner's extensive modern-art collection.

The perimeter offices function as multiuse private studies with desk and computer workspace, and research, filing, and storage areas. Informal seating and formal conference tables reflect the organization's creative-productive work ethic.

top: main circulation gallery off elevator lobby, bottom: typical perimeter associate's office from corridor

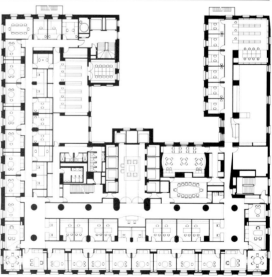

top: partner's office, bottom left: associate's office, bottom right: plan

partner's office and conference room

International Design Center
Long Island City, New York
1986–1987

Herman Miller Showroom

top: entry from public balcony, bottom: entry kiosk and reception

view through entry kiosk

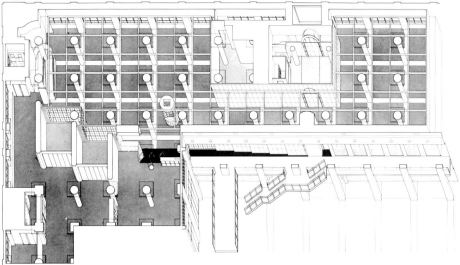

top: showroom looking toward public gallery, bottom: axonometric

The parti of the Herman Miller showroom provides a flexible design to allow frequent spatial and display changes while maintaining a constant sense of presence. The 21,000-square-foot loft space is on the second floor of Center I in the International Design Center. The showroom is 13 feet 6 inches high with a raised mezzanine floor along its southern edge. Three-foot-diameter concrete columns mark the loft space at twenty-foot intervals. In addition to the display areas, the showroom contains a sixty-seat multiuse audiovisual meeting space, conference room, pantry, manager's office, staff workstations, and extensive storage space.

A custom-designed lighting grid defines the principal showroom areas. Suspended from the existing ceiling, the ten-foot-square grid establishes a second horizontal plane for accent lighting, display panels, and hanging fabric. The showroom's permanent materials include white neoparium, which defines the audiovisual room as a gridded object in the plan-field, frosted and clear glass in the offices and meeting rooms, painted millwork, and Formica cabinets. Juxtaposed with the sandblasted concrete columns and perimeter shear walls, the material palette is a constant reference to the overall planning grid.

detail view of stair to second level

detail of ceiling lighting grid and display

left: textile display wall, right: conference room

typical area in showroom

lecture-seminar room

New York, New York
1987–1988

The Georgetown Group, Inc.

reception-waiting space

A dual identity characterizes the 5,000-square-foot project for this real estate management-investment firm. The L-shaped plan's pivotal volume is a circular conference room that functions both as an open, public pavilion and a closed, private room. Sliding curved door-walls form a cylindrical volume when closed, or reveal a corner view from the circulation and work spaces when opened.

The offices also include a reception-waiting area, a second conference room, three executive offices, three associate offices, four secretarial stations, and support space. Cherry and ebonized oak, linen walls, and carpeted floors, along with the craft aesthetic of the furniture, support the intended calm of the environment.

conference room

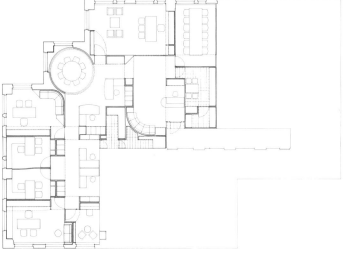

top: partner's office, bottom: floor plan

top and bottom: president's office

New York, New York
1987–1988

This 42,000-square-foot office for a record and music-publishing company occupies the top two floors of a typical Sixth Avenue office building. The plan is organized around a two-story entry and reception space with a granite and oak cylindrical stair connecting the elevator lobbies and the internal corridor-gallery spaces to perimeter offices.

Multiple solid, transparent, and translucent planes delineate heirarchical spaces along the circulation galleries.

Partners' offices are designed as loft volumes with panoramic views, accommodating specific programmatic requirements.

The architectural dynamics are intensified by a sensory awareness of the music produced by the company's clients. The design ethic of the space supports and encourages the creative community it houses.

SBK Entertainment World, Inc.

top: entry-reception space, bottom: reception space from stair

main stair

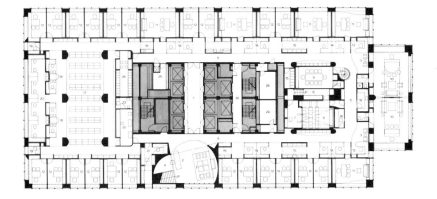

top: president's office, bottom: plan of forty-second floor

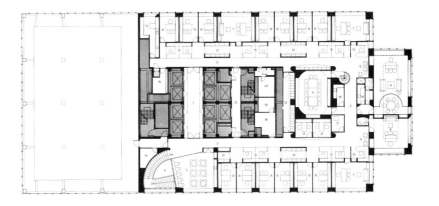

top: president's office, bottom: plan of forty-third floor

top: northwest interior corner, bottom: typical secretary workstations and circulation corridor

top: main conference room, bottom: screening room

This large advertising company's new facilities are dispersed over fourteen contiguous floors. The organization of the program resulted in a parti that allows horizontal and vertical variation within a system of spatial repetition from floor to floor. A cohesive aesthetic matrix is established by using materials and colors to articulate public spaces such as elevator lobbies, stairs, and circulation galleries.

One of the 300,000-square-foot facility's most unique spatial configurations is a double-height exhibition, meeting, and reception volume between the diagonal trusses on the eighth and ninth floors. A stair and stacked conference rooms overlook the space, providing a visual counterpoint to the diagonal trusses. The articulation of this public component, adjacent to the executive and creative floors, is the core of the design.

D'Arcy Masius Benton & Bowles, Inc.

left: typical elevator lobby, right: exhibition space from stair

exhibition space and stair

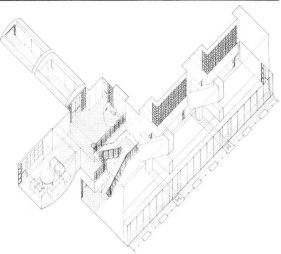

top: typical conference room overlooking exhibition space, bottom left: exhibition space, bottom right: axonometric of exhibition space

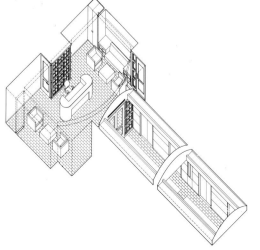

top: typical reception-waiting space, bottom left: axonometric of typical reception-waiting space, bottom right: typical executive corridor

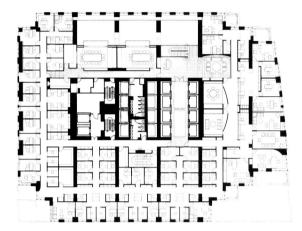
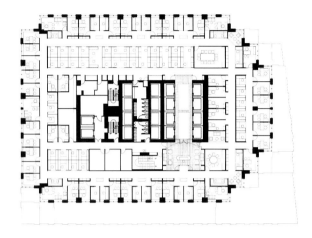
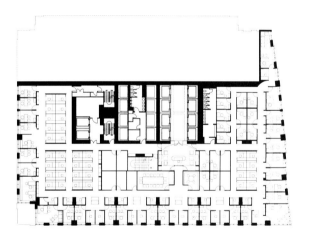
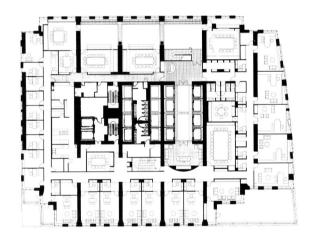

typical floor plans

typical executive secretary workstation

New York, New York
1990

These offices occupy a linear space of 10,000 square feet on the forty-second floor of a building overlooking Central Park. The space was designed to display both a private art collection and a Vienna Secessionist furniture collection. The project's aesthetic image supports the history of the art objects and the goals of the organization's separate entities.

A skylighted gallery—the major organizational space—leads from the entry-reception space through a layer of open workstations to a rotunda, terminating the gallery promenade. The rotunda serves as a foyer to a private suite containing an office, dining room, and library. Entered directly from the gallery, the perimeter offices repeat the material vocabulary of the public spaces to extend the spatial layering to the window wall. The materials and colors, wood base moldings, integrated door and wall systems, and hierarchical notations in the cabinetwork define the overall aesthetic, integrating historical components with an abstracted, interpretive, three-dimensional collage.

Offices for Ronald S. Lauder

top: entry-waiting space, bottom: typical workstations from exhibition gallery

exhibition gallery from rotunda

top: rotunda, bottom: private dining room

top: main conference room, bottom: plan

West Los Angeles, California
1991–1992

This two-floor, 45,000-square-foot office for a pension management and investment firm responds to the client's egalitarian vision. On both floors the four corners are designated as common spaces—conference rooms, cafeteria, library, and board-meeting room—leaving four perimeter zones on each floor, to be divided into equal-sized offices.

A two-story entry and reception space is articulated by an open stair to a glass-block bridge that connects with circulation galleries filled with contemporary art. Natural light penetrates the galleries from interior clerestory windows in the office walls. Adjacent to the galleries are open workstations and another layer of file and support space.

The perimeter offices were designed for maximum efficiency and flexibility. An integrated cabinet and millwork system of wood paneling and translucent and transparent glass establishes the aesthetic of the entire space.

The Capital Group

top: entry-reception space, bottom: second-level entry bridge

217

entry-reception space and bridge from stair

typical corner of public corridor

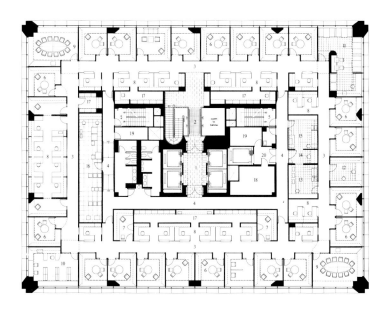

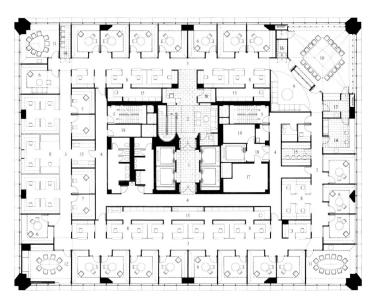

left: fifteenth-floor and sixteenth-floor plans, top right: typical secretary workstations, bottom right: typical public corridor

top: conference room waiting-reception area, bottom: main conference room

top: statistics workstation area, bottom: typical associate's office

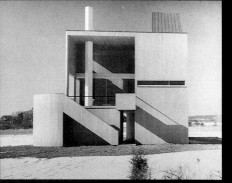

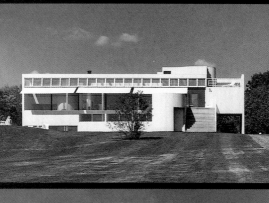

*...earlier work, from top: 1965 Gwathmey Residence; 1971 Cogan Residence;
1977 Taft Residence; 1979 deMenil Residence*

Residential Buildings and Projects

New York, New York
1983–1985

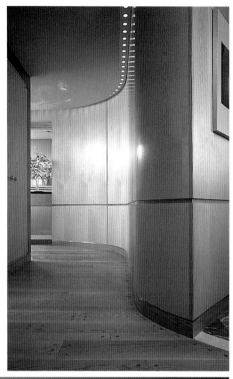

This 2,500-square-foot apartment is located on the fifty-second floor of a prominent midtown tower with spectacular views of Central Park and the city. A pavilion in the sky was carved out of the existing low-ceilinged space, creating a calm, dense, and introspective environment.

Two domains, public and private, are defined in the apartment. The public domain, or pavilion, is a continuous, interconnected volume housing an entry foyer-gallery, bar-study, kitchen, and living-dining space. Its materials—oak and marble floors, ash paneling and cabinetwork, oak doors and trim, and plaster ceilings—are used in a system of layers in plan and section. The private domain, composed of two bedroom-and-bath suites, is distinguished by the introduction of local symmetry and a sense of closure. The spatial intervention is reinforced by layers of wood frames and curtains on the window wall, which create multiple planes of transparency, translucency, and opacity along the perimeter.

Spielberg Apartment

top: entry foyer, bottom: bar-den with living room beyond

living-dining room with piano bar beyond

living room

top: master bedroom from hall, bottom left: plan, bottom right: master bedroom

Kent, Connecticut
1983–1988

Garey Residence

south facade with main entry from driveway

Designed as an object in the woods, the Garey Residence is gradually revealed by a circulation system that begins at the private driveway and culminates in the glass-enclosed, cylindrical living space. The path leads through the site, into the house, and eventually back out to the landscape, with views of a mountain stream and forest. The massing changes from solid (public) to void (private) as the split-level plan responds to the landscape, reinforcing the dialogue between architecture and nature.

The lower ground floor houses the entry and garage. The upper ground floor, one half-level above, contains the kitchen-dining area, the sitting room, and the two-and-a-half-story living room. Over the garage—a half-level above the living area—is the two-bedroom children's wing. Another half-level above, overlooking the living space, is the master bedroom suite, which extends one more half-level to a study and roof deck over the children's wing. The split-level plan integrates the site's natural slope and responds to the client's desire for privacy, thereby refining a familiar house parti within new parameters.

east facade from woods

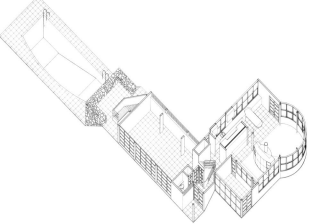

top: kitchen-dining room, bottom: ground-level axonometric

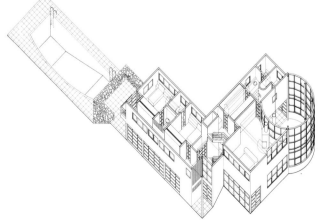

top left: living room-sitting room, top right: master bedroom, bottom: second-level axonometric

living room

233

top: living room with dining room beyond, bottom: east facade

view of stair from second level

top left: master bathroom, top right: detail of second-level gallery, bottom: master bedroom

East Hampton, New York
1985–1987

The Spielberg Residence combines historical references and modernist ideals in a relocated eighteenth-century Dutch barn on a site in East Hampton. The strategy of the renovation-transformation was to maintain the frame's structural and volumetric integrity. The exterior is clad in wood shingles that transform its scale and image to that of the area's vernacular architecture, but maintain the barn's iconic volume. The interior reveals the barn's structure by using new stucco walls and the exposed frame to create a half-timbered exterior reading.

The symmetry of the house is reflected in the landscape. Between the barn and a new gatehouse is a pear-tree courtyard that reflects the plan dimensions of the barn. The overall figure-ground transformation is structured by three spatial experiences: the passage from the driveway to the auto court; the gatehouse passageway to the pear-tree courtyard, which uses biaxial symmetry to anchor the rotation of the house and gatehouse on the site; and finally, the frontality and cross-axial interior of the barn.

Spielberg Residence

left: eighteenth-century Dutch barn frame, right: view from west across pond

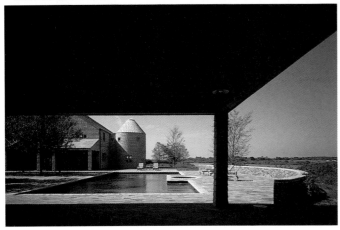

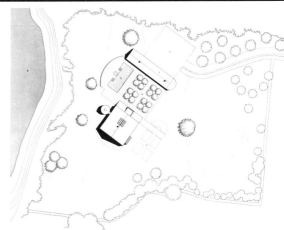

top: north facade from pear-tree courtyard, bottom left: view from pool porch, bottom right: site plan

living room

top: living room from study, bottom: entry hall

top: living room, bottom: dining room

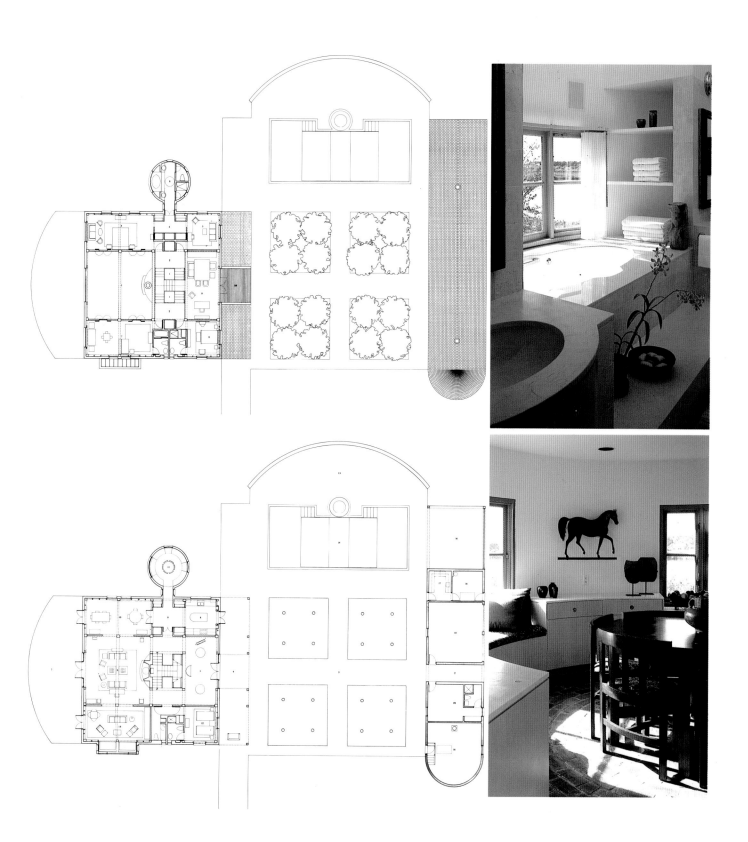

left: ground-level plan, second-level plan, top right: master bathroom, bottom right: breakfast room

Shelburne Farms
Shelburne, Vermont
1985–1987

Opel Residence

south facade from access road

Located on six acres in the historic Shelburne Farms estate, the Opel Residence is sited on a gently rolling, wooded peninsula on Lake Champlain, with views of the Adirondack Mountains to the west. The house was conceived as a composite object, rather than a single volume, in order to provide separate dwellings for three generations of a large family. A main house for the parents, two guest house-pavilions for their grown children, and a bunkhouse for the grandchildren articulate the programmatic elements. Outdoor spaces are linked by a covered arcade parallel to the lake.

The circulation sequence begins at the auto court, which is set in a maple grove at the south end of the arcade. After passing between the garage and the entry to the children's bunkhouse above, the arcade opens to a lakeside pool terrace, then leads to the two guest-house entries opposite the garden, and finally arrives, on the north end, at the entry to the main house.

Within the main house, a two-story entry-stair hall, two-and-a-half-story living space, kitchen-breakfast room, and dining space all have views of the lake. A studio overlooks the living space from the first half-level above, with a master bedroom suite on the second level. Each guest house also faces the lake, with an entry-stair hall, two-and-a-half-story dining-living space, kitchen, and adjacent courtyard. A sleeping balcony and bathroom occupy the second level, over the arcade.

This design exploration resulted in a newfound house parti. In its collection of architecturally defined outdoor spaces and house volumes distinguished by their roof forms and silhouettes, the building addresses the scale of the site and refers to its historical typology, while sensitively defining the private domains.

detail of east facade

west facade from Lake Champlain

bottom left: section through guest house, bottom right: section through main-house living room and studio

top: west facade from pool terrace, bottom left: detail of south facade, bottom right: site plan

guest house west facade

guest-house living-dining space

left: main-house living room, right: main-house living room from stair

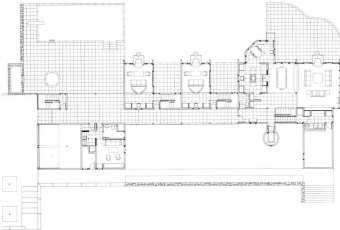

top: main-house living and dining spaces from entry hall,   bottom: ground-level plan

top left: entry hall from living room, top right: dressing room, middle right: studio, bottom: second-level plan

East Hampton, New York*
1986–1989

Differences in orientation and landscape elevations from north to south on the four-acre oceanfront site are reflected in the two distinct facades of this house in East Hampton. The program includes a main house, pool, tennis court, and caretaker's house.

Asymmetrical circulation, integrating building and landscape design, is layered in both north-south and east-west axes. The driveway is bounded on the west by a row of cypress trees and on the east by a double hedge. It forms a south axis with views of the Atlantic Ocean through a pear-tree courtyard. The three-story north facade of the main house anchors the site as an entry wall and implied gateway to the dune and ocean beyond. The two-story south facade fronts the ocean with a brise-soleil frame of asymmetrical planes and spaces that contrasts with the solid north facade. The main entry stair to the site and the house traverses the level change in the landscape, creating a sense of scale and place reminiscent of nineteenth-century ocean villas in Newport and Southampton.

Steinberg Residence

west facade from pool terrace

south facade from dune

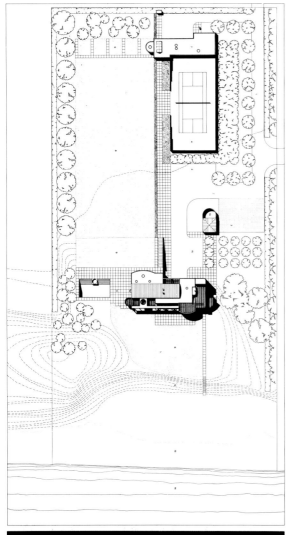

top left: site plan, bottom left: south facade from beach

north facade

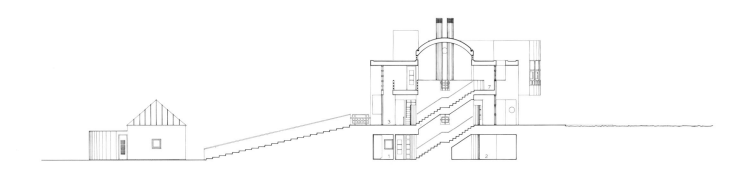

top: deck off children's bedrooms, bottom: section through stair

southeast corner

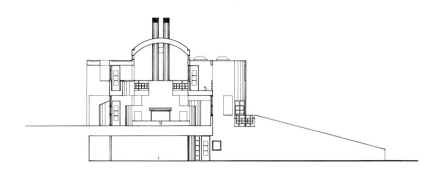

top: east facade from pear-tree courtyard,   bottom left: detail of east exterior stair,   bottom right: section through living room

living room

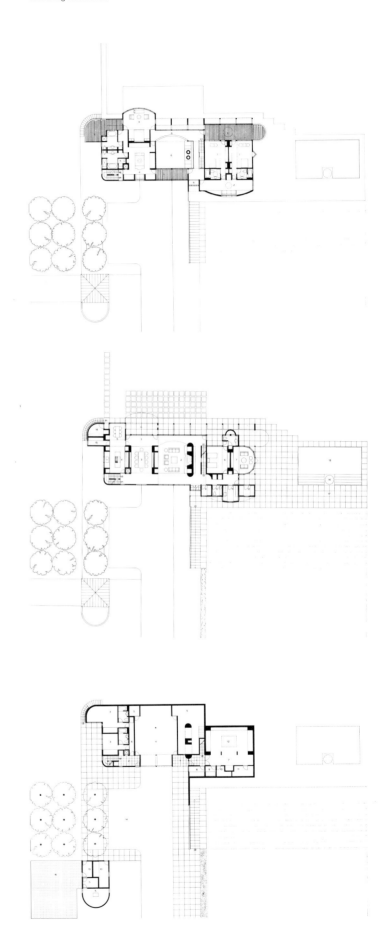

top left: second-level stair balcony, bottom left: entry hall, right: ground-level, second-level, third-level plans

top left: dressing room, top right: children's bedroom, bottom: master bedroom

New York, New York
1988–1991

The Gwathmey Apartment represents the transformation of a typical 2,500-square-foot Fifth Avenue apartment into a spatially complex pavilion loft with a design that summarizes ideas and provokes further investigations.

A contrapuntal balance between stable and dynamic spaces is expressed by asymmetrical plan manipulations that emphasize the exterior window walls and recenter the interior facades. The space appears to have been carved rather than assembled, juxtaposing a sense of weight and density with the openness of the plan.

Architect-designed objects collected over time allude to historical design preferences and serve as reference points in the object-space dynamic of the parti. The material palette reinforces the programmatic and volumetric manipulation, adding to the sense of collage while supporting the hierarchical articulation of details.

Gwathmey Apartment

gallery from entry

detail of fireplace wall

sitting-living room

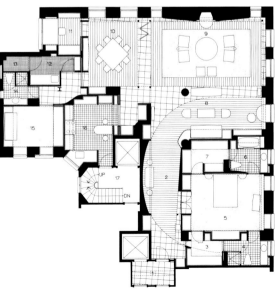

left: dining room from living room, top right: gallery from living room, bottom right: floor plan

The 150-foot-wide site parallels a highway on the north and the ocean on the south. Private residences border the property on the east and west. The parti combines the typologies of a row house and a courtyard house, creating a hierarchy of building volumes and outdoor spaces that layer the site from north to south and result in a literal and psychological transformation from highway to beach.

Borrowing from the row-house typology, the highway facade of the entry building is the first layer on the site. It is primarily solid, rendered as a carved, abstract horizontal wall punctured by an entry gate. The ground level houses a screening room, guest house, garage, and pool support space. The second level contains two children's bedrooms, a playroom, and a caretaker's apartment over the garage.

Transition from the entry layer to the main house employs an element of the second typology—a pear-tree courtyard—defined on the east by the second site layer, a building that contains a kitchen, pantry, and breakfast room on the ground level and a master bathroom with dressing and exercise areas on the second level. The courtyard is defined on the west by a bridge connecting the children's wing to the main house on the second level.

The main house, the third site layer, contains a living room, dining room, library, and porch on the ground level. On the second level a master bedroom, study, and decks face the ocean, overlooking the two-and-a-half-story living space.

A pool terrace extends the open space of the pear-tree courtyard under the bridge, west of the main house and south of the entry building, where it is joined by an ocean terrace to the beach below. Modulated by paved areas and lawn, the ocean terrace forms the fourth layer from the east edge to the west edge of the site. Intersections of multiple layers of building and space create a complex balance of solid and void, in the referential cubist tradition of our work.

Oceanfront Residence

southwest corner of main house

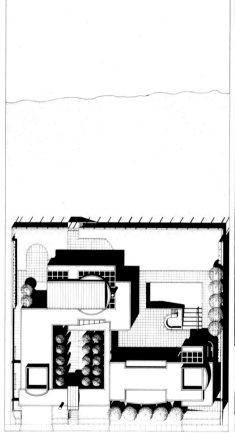

top: south facade from beach, bottom left: site plan, bottom right: southwest corner of entry building guest room and playroom

top: view from southwest, bottom: main house fireplace from pool terrace

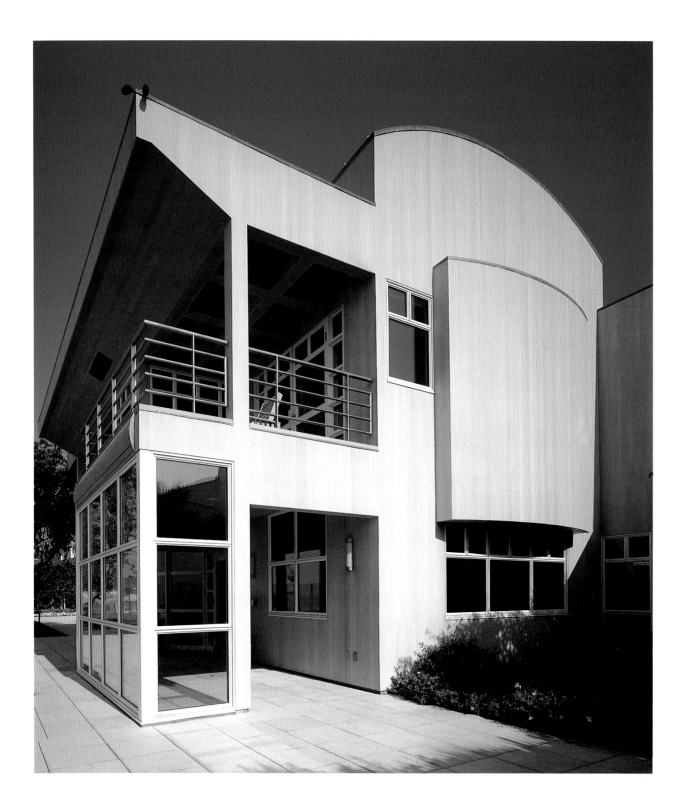

southeast corner of main house

top left: living room, bottom left: main house corner at pool terrace, top right: living room from balcony, bottom right: living room from entry

living room from dining area

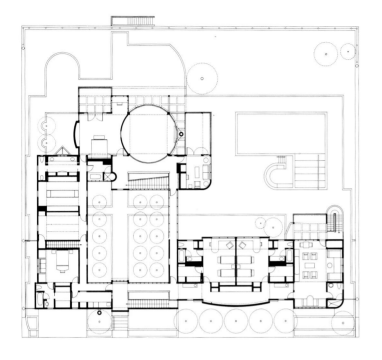

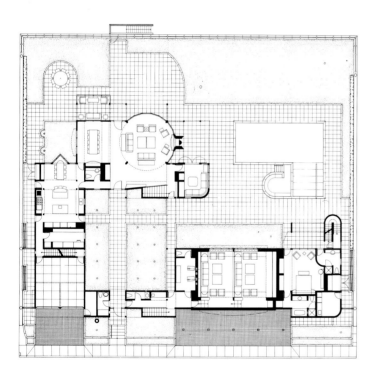

left: ground-level plan, second-level plan, top right: main house stair from balcony, bottom right: gallery and stair from entry

living-dining area from balcony

left: master bedroom, top and bottom right: screening room

Zumikon, Switzerland
1990–1992

The design for this residence was dictated by its steeply sloping site with views to Lake Zurich and the Alps to the south. The massing resulted from a modernist interpretation of a restrictive zoning ordinance that affected the building's aesthetic as well as its height above grade. Outdoor spaces and roofs function as terraces to the interconnected building masses in the house-as-village parti.

The building element to the south contains a garage and a two-and-a-half-story public entry on the lowest level. An open stair extends the entry vertically, and an art and sculpture gallery extends it horizontally to the family stair in the three-story space to the north. The second level of the south element contains a kitchen-breakfast room, servants' quarters, and service entry. A public stair landing leads to a sculpture-pool terrace and gallery parallel to the dining space, a library-sitting room, and a two-and-a-half-story living volume in the north element. A master bedroom suite crowns the north element, adjacent to the dining roof terrace and two floors of children's bedrooms.

The parti incorporates formal propositions explored in both the Opel and California residences. Here, however, the sloping site and the poured-concrete construction technology impart a new physical and psychological sense of density and permanence.

Bechtler Residence

east facade under construction

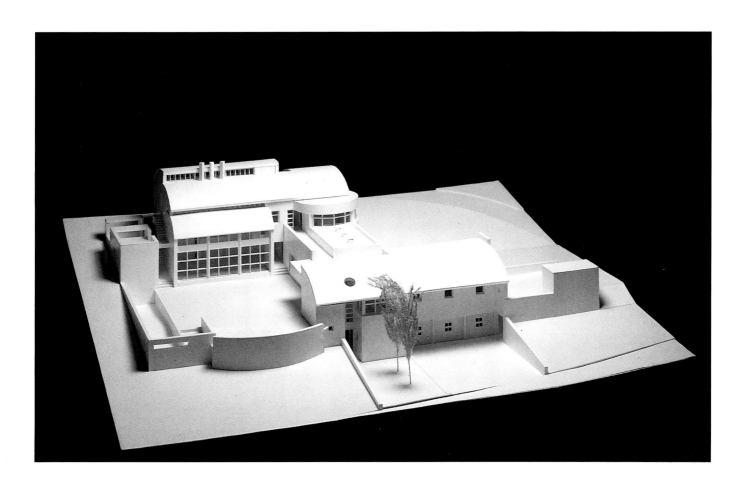

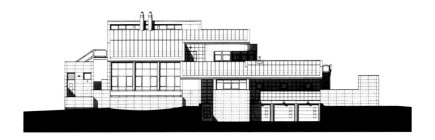

top: aerial view of model from south, bottom: south elevation

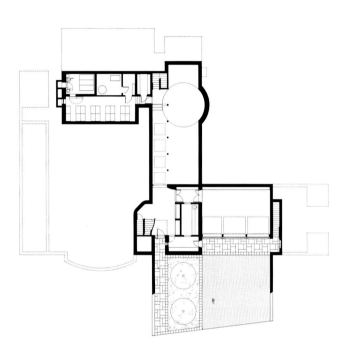
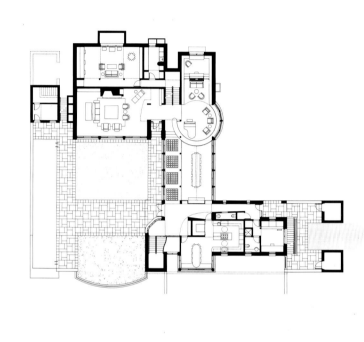
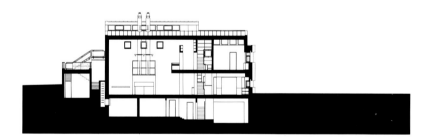
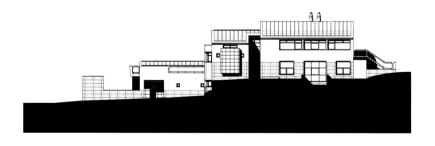

top: ground-level plan, second-level plan, bottom: section through living room, north elevation

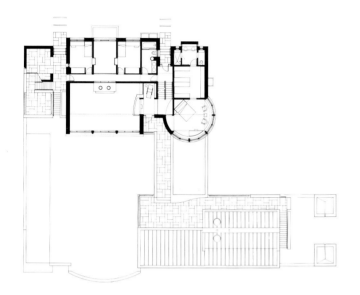
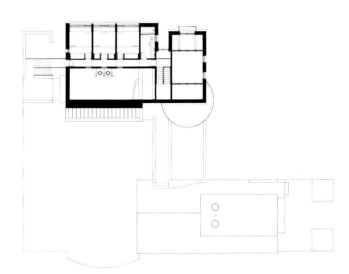

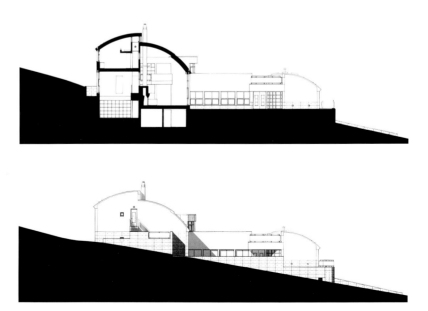

top: third-level plan, fourth-level plan, bottom: section through living room and children's spaces, west elevation

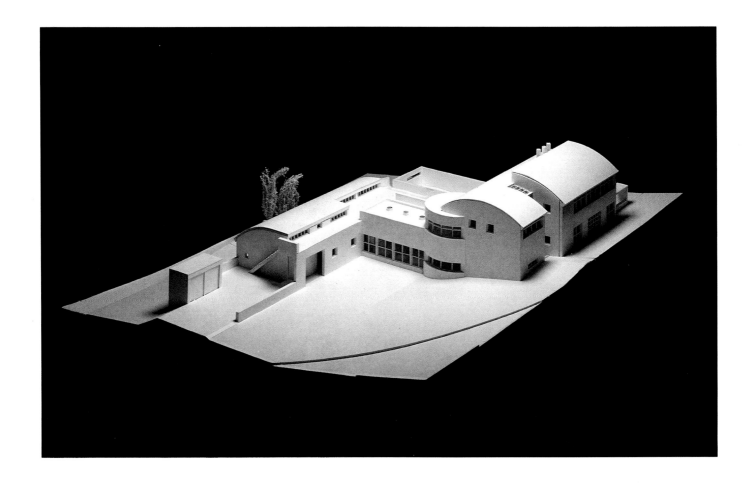

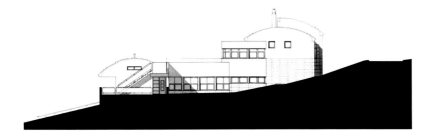

top: aerial view of model from northeast, bottom: east elevation

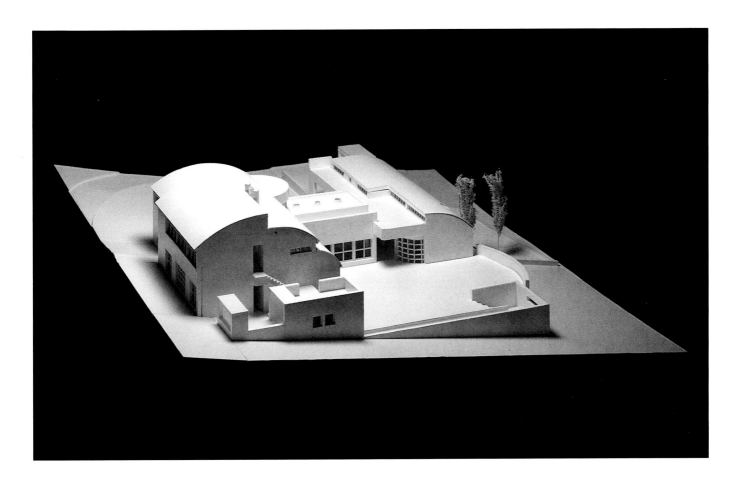

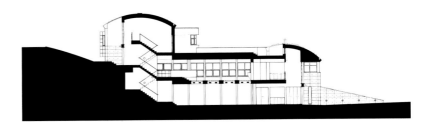

top: aerial view of model from northwest, bottom: longitudinal section through gallery-dining room and main stair

Taipei, Taiwan
1990–1994

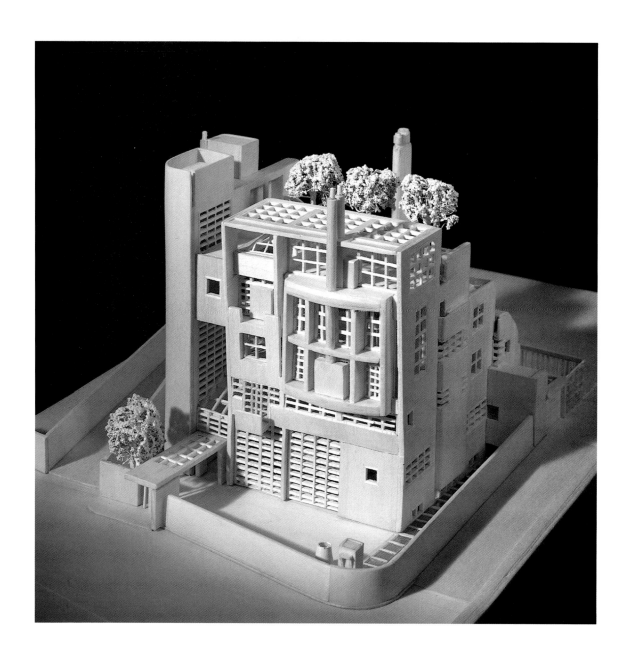

Chen Residence

south facade of model

north facade of model

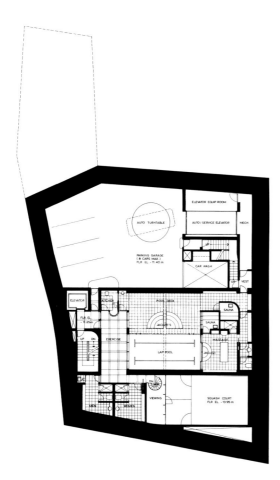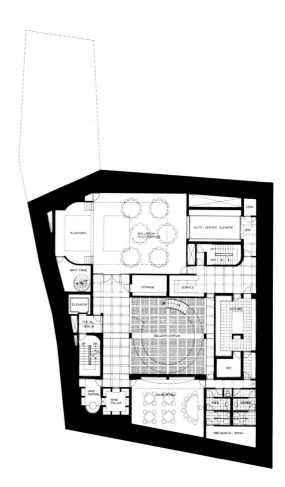

Chinese cultural tradition—specifically, the separation of private and public domains in family life—influenced the parti of this house. The building massing on this 10,000-square-foot sloping, suburban site is strictly defined vertically and horizontally by zoning regulations. Thus, the 40,000-square-foot program required a unique organizational strategy. The site is enclosed by a volcanic stone wall defining a two-level garden (public below and private above) as the parti's referential space.

The public entry leads to a four-and-a-half-story gallery that visually extends the garden below grade with a two-story south-facing glass wall and grand stair. The private entry overlooks the gallery and public entry from a balcony on the north side. It leads to both the stair and elevator core, as well as a ramp-bridge across the gallery to two guest units on the intermediate half-level.

As though it were excavated from the gallery, the private house extends five stories above grade, becoming the object in the garden. The second floor contains three children's bedrooms, the grandmother's bedroom and sitting space, a music room, a playroom, and an outdoor stair to the private garden below. The third floor contains a two-story living room, dining room, kitchen and breakfast room, and a teppanyaki room,

lower-level basement plan, middle-level basement plan

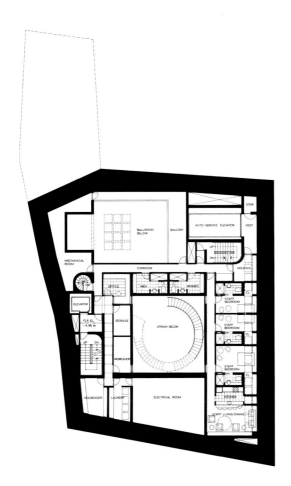

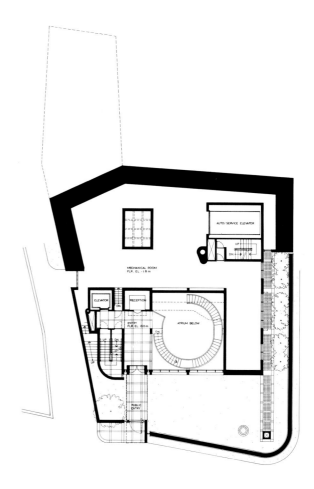

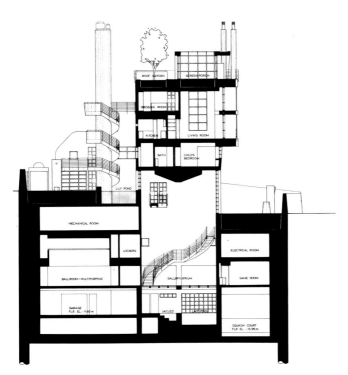

top: first-level basement plan, public-entry ground-level plan, bottom: section

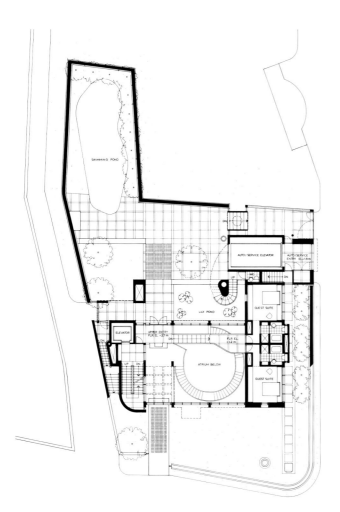

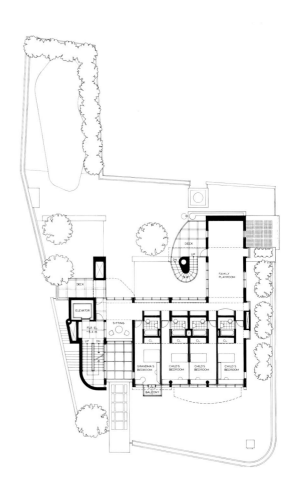

which leads to a terrace and outdoor stair to the private garden. The fourth floor contains the master bedroom suite, sitting room, study, and Jacuzzi terrace, which also leads down a stair to the private garden. The fifth-floor roof contains a screened moon room and roof-garden terrace with panoramic views of Taipei. The ceremonial aspect of the garden terrace resurrects the modernist roof-as-new-ground-plane ethic.

Built out to the limits of the site, the underground program occupies four levels. The lower levels are reached from the entry gallery, with its glass-block floor and recirculating water wall, and from a large service elevator and stair. They contain a ballroom and theater space, game-room, bar and wine cellar, full-service kitchen and ancillary service spaces, as well as a squash court, spa, and six-car garage.

The private house is 11,000 square feet and the public-entertainment house, 30,000 square feet. The project transforms a comprehensive program on a restricted site into a spatially complex and concentrated structure that is at once urban and rural, contextual and self-referential, encompassing a philosophy of modern architectural principles.

top: private-entry ground-level plan, second-level plan

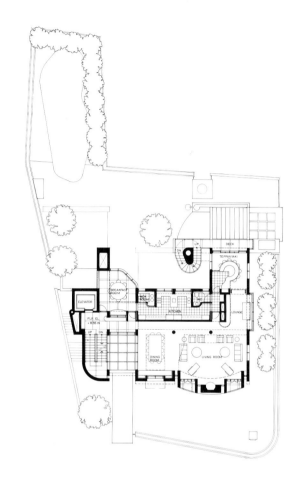

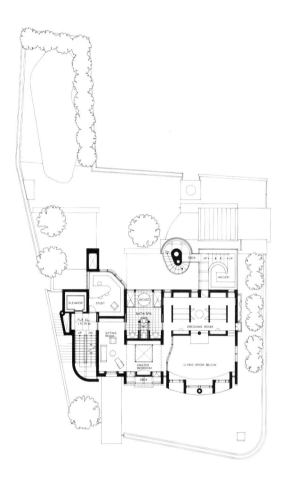

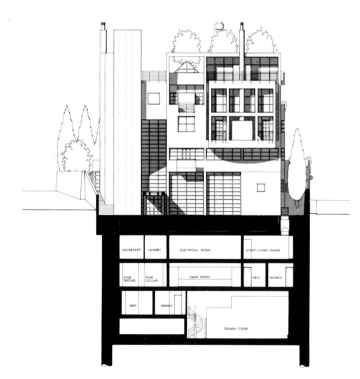

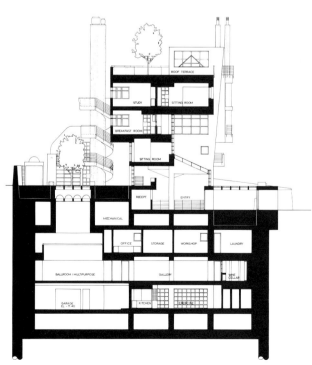

top: third-level plan, fourth-level plan, bottom: south elevation, section

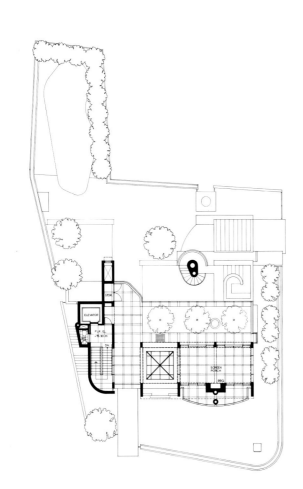
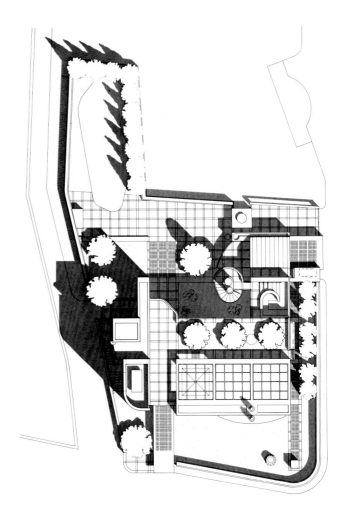

roof-level plan, site plan

east facade of model

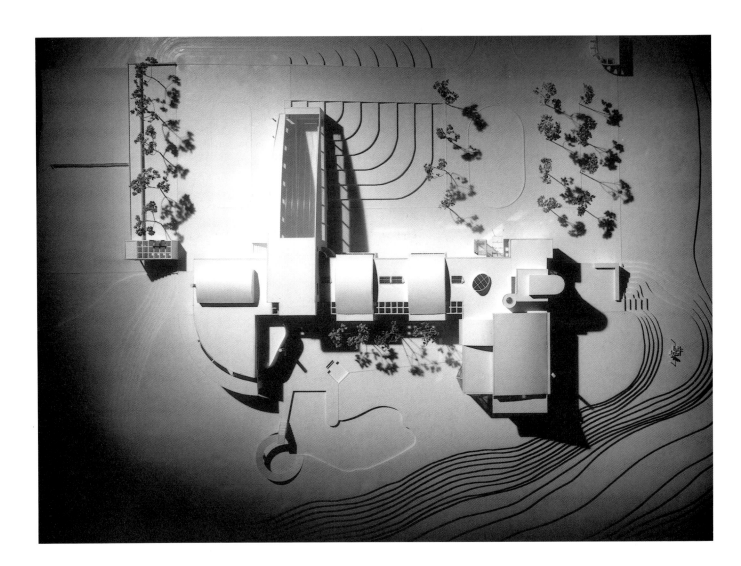

Sited atop an 85-acre foothill, with panoramic views north to the lakes, east to the plains, and south to the capital city, the parti is a compilation of typologies.

The building defines the site by its horizontal extension on the west entry facade, by a lower-level and an upper-level entry court, on the south by a lower-level play court, and on the east by an expansive lawn and pool terrace engaging a two-story covered arcade that connects the main house on the north and the entertainment-guest house on the south.

Multiple building and site layers, horizontal and vertical circulation systems, and the hierarchically articulated massing recall strategies employed in the Taft, Opel, and Oceanfront residences. The resulting collage assemblage is read in fragments as well as holistically, changing scale and objectness simultaneously. If, in fact, our residences are archetypal investigations, then Villa Austin is truly representative.

Villa Austin

aerial view of model

top: aerial view from northeast, bottom: northeast corner

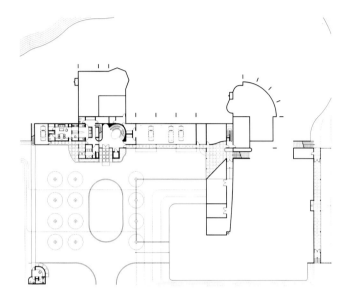
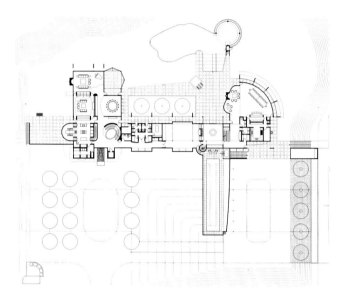

top: ground-level and first-level plans,   bottom: section

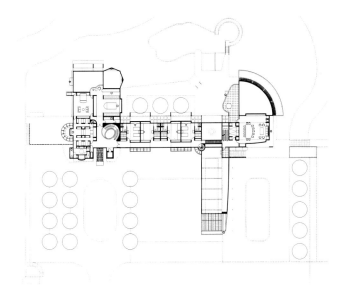
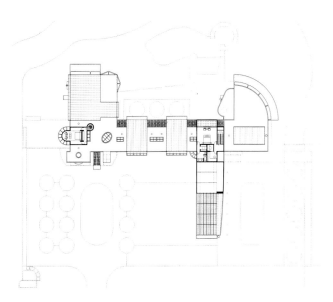

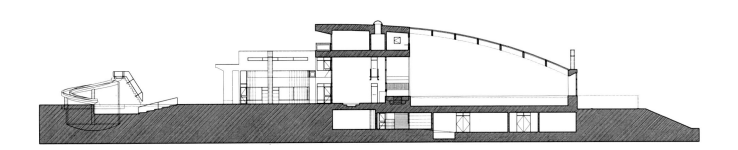

top: second-level and third-level plans, bottom: section through indoor pool

top: aerial view from southeast, bottom: southeast corner

top: aerial view from northwest, bottom: northwest corner

Charles Gwathmey, Architect

1964   Miller Residence
Fire Island, New York

1965   Herlinger–Bristol Ltd.
Showrooms and Offices
New York, New York

Gwathmey Residence and Studio
Amagansett, New York

Gwathmey & Henderson, Architects

1966   Straus Residence
Purchase, New York

1967   Sedacca Residence
East Hampton, New York

Goldberg Residence
Manchester, Connecticut

Buildings, Projects, Furniture, and Objects, 1964–1992

1968

Cooper Residence
Orleans, Massachusetts

Gwathmey, Henderson, and Siegel Architects

Steel Residences I & II
Bridgehampton, New York

Thomas Pritchard, Christopher Chimera, James Swan,
Timothy Wood

Service Building and Heating Plant
State University of New York at Purchase
Purchase, New York

Durwood Herron, Timothy Wood

1969

Dunaway Apartment
New York, New York

James Swan, Thomas Pritchard, Timothy Wood

Brooklyn Friends School
Brooklyn, New York

Andrew Petit, Stephen Potters, Timothy Wood

Dormitory, Dining, and Student Union Building
State University of New York at Purchase
Purchase, New York

Andrew Petit, Durwood Herron, Stephen Potters,
Thomas Pritchard, Timothy Wood

Gwathmey Siegel Architects

Gwathmey Siegel Architects
Offices
New York, New York

1970

Eskilson Residence (project)
Roxbury, Connecticut

Timothy Wood, James Swan

Whig Hall
Princeton University
Princeton, New Jersey

Timothy Wood, Stephen Potters, James Swan

Tolan Residence
Amagansett, New York

Timothy Wood

1971

New York Apartment
New York, New York

Timothy Wood, Stephen Potters

Cogan Residence
East Hampton, New York

Timothy Wood

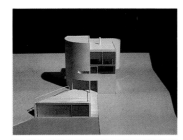

Elia-Bash Residence
Califon, New Jersey

Timothy Wood

1972

Cohn Residence
Amagansett, New York

Timothy Wood, Marvin Mitchell

Whitney Road Housing
Perinton, New York

Marvin Mitchell, John Choi, Susan Green, Timothy Wood

1973

Gwathmey Barn
Greenwich, Connecticut

Timothy Wood, Stephen Potters

Pearl's Restaurant
New York, New York

John Chimera

Sagner Residence (project)
West Orange, New Jersey

Ivan Zaknic, John Chimera

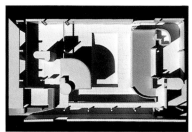

Geffen Residence (project)
Malibu, California

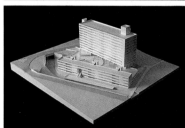

St. Casmir Housing (project)
Yonkers, New York

Peter Szilagyi, Marvin Mitchell, Ivan Zaknic

1974

Buettner Residence
Sloatsburg, New York

Peter Szilagyi

Transammonia Corporation
Offices
New York, New York

John Chimera, Peter Szilagyi

Charof Residence
Montauk, New York

Peter Szilagyi, Ivan Zaknic

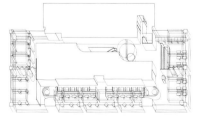

Four Seasons Restaurant (project)
Nagoya, Japan

John Chimera

303

Kislevitz Residence
Westhampton, New York

Peter Szilagyi, John Chimera, Ivan Zaknic

Vidal Sassoon
Salon
La Costa, California

Tsun-Kin Tam, Gustav Rosenlof

Vidal Sassoon
Salon
New York, New York

Tsun-Kin Tam, Gustav Rosenlof

Vidal Sassoon
Salon
Chicago, Illinios

Tsun-Kin Tam, Gustav Rosenlof

Vidal Sassoon
Salon
Beverly Hills, California

Tsun-Kin Tam, Gustav Rosenlof

Vidal Sassoon
Corporate Offices
Los Angeles, California

Tsun-Kin Tam, David Murphy

1975   Student Apartment Housing
State University of New York at Purchase
Purchase, New York

Marvin Mitchell, Gustav Rosenlof, Peter Szilagyi, Tsun-Kin Tam

Nassau County Art Center (project)
Roslyn, New York

One Times Square (project)
Office Building
New York, New York

Peter Szilagyi, Gustav Rosenlof, Tsun-Kin Tam, Ivan Zaknic

Island Walk Cooperative Housing
Reston, Virginia

Marvin Mitchell, Jose Coriano, Eleanor Klein, Gustav Rosenlof,
Tsun-Kin Tam

Bower and Gardner
Law Offices
New York, New York

Peter Szilagyi, Margaret Jann, Gustav Rosenlof

The Evans Partnership
Prototype Office Building

Richard Gould, Gustav Rosenlof

The Evans Partnership
Office Building
Piscataway, New Jersey

Richard Gould, Marvin Mitchell
Rotwein & Blake Associated Architects, P.A.
(Associate Architect)

Unger Apartment
New York, New York

Peter Szilagyi, Gustav Rosenlof, Tsun-Kin Tam

Damson Oil Corporation
Office Building
Houston, Texas

Marvin Mitchell, Gustav Rosenlof, David Murphy

U.S. Steakhouse Restaurant
New York, New York

Gustav Rosenlof

Northpoint Office Building
Houston, Texas

George Wu, Ivan Zaknic

Barber Oil Corporation
Offices
New York, New York

Tsun-Kin Tam, Jose Coriano, David Murphy

1976

East Campus Student Housing and Academic Center
Columbia University
New York, New York

Joel Bargmann, Robert Anderson, Jose Coriano, Steven Harris,
Karen Jacobson, Andrew Minchun, Vincent Mulcahey
Emery Roth & Sons, P.C. (Associate Architect)

Haupt Residence
Amagansett, New York

Peter Szilagyi, Margaret Jann, Gustav Rosenlof

Weitz Residence
Quogue, New York

Peter Szilagyi, Margaret Jann, Gustav Rosenlof, Edward Walsh

Thomas & Betts Corporation
Office Building
Raritan, New Jersey

Richard Gould, David Murphy, Marvin Mitchell

Benenson Residence
Rye, New York

Peter Szilagyi, Eleanor Klein, Edward Walsh

Swirl, Inc.
Showrooms and Offices
New York, New York

Gustav Rosenlof

Hyatt Hotel and Casino (project)
Aruba, Netherlands Antilles

Andrew Minchun, Marvin Mitchell, Gustav Rosenlof,
Tsun-Kin Tam, Ivan Zaknic

Swid Apartment I
New York, New York

Peter Szilagyi, Jose Coriano, Margaret Jann

1977

Poster Originals, Ltd.
New York, New York

Peter Szilagyi

Garey Shirtmakers
Showrooms and Offices
New York, New York

John Colamarino

Crowley Residence
Greenwich, Connecticut

Peter Szilagyi, George Wu, Ivan Zaknic

Geffen Apartment
New York, New York

Jose Coriano

Belkin Memorial Room
Yeshiva University
New York, New York

John Colamarino, Marvin Mitchell

Taft Residence
Cincinnati, Ohio

Gustav Rosenlof, Karen Jacobson, George Wu

Northgate Housing (project)
Roosevelt Island, New York

Jacob Alspector, Steven Harris, Michael Monsky,
Vincent Mulcahey, Edward Walsh

Lincoln Center for the Performing Arts
Adminstrative Offices
New York, New York

Tsun-Kin Tam, Jose Coriano, Vincent Mulcahey

FDM Productions
Offices
New York, New York

David Murphy, Edward Walsh, Jose Coriano

AT&T Office Building
Parsippany, New Jersey

Richard Gould, Mark Simon
Rotwein & Blake Associated Architects, P. A.
(Associate Architect)

The Evans Partnership
Office Building and Offices
Parsippany, New Jersey

Richard Gould, Jose Coriano, David Murphy
Rotwein & Blake Associated Architects, P.A.
(Associate Architect)

The Evans Partnership
Offices
New York, New York

Gustav Rosenlof, David Murphy, Tsun-Kin Tam, Ivan Zaknic

Gwathmey Siegel & Associates Architects
In project teams, italics indicate associate in charge

1978   Amax Petroleum Corporation
Office Building
Houston, Texas

George Wu

Knoll International
Showroom and Office Building
Boston, Massachusetts

Jacob Alspector, John Colamarino, David Hingston,
David Murphy, Nick Toecheff

Sycamore Place
Elderly Housing
Columbus, Indiana

Jacob Alspector, Lynn Bensel, Glen Fries, William Garbus,
Dean Marchetto, Joseph Ruocco

Pence Street
Family Housing
Columbus, Indiana

Jacob Alspector, Margaret Fitzpatrick, Lynn Bensel,
Jose Coriano, William Garbus, Dirk Kramer, Dean Marchetto,
Joseph Ruocco, Irene Torroella

Shezan Restaurant
New York, New York

David Murphy, Margaret Jann

Giorgio Armani, Inc.
Showrooms and Offices
New York, New York

Joel Bargmann, Jose Coriano

1979

Library and Science Building
Westover School
Middlebury, Connecticut

Jacob Alspector, Paul Aferiat, Richard Clarke,
Howard Goldstein, Richard Gould, David Knowlton,
Thomas Whitrock

Hines Residence (project)
Martha's Vineyard, Massachusetts

Gustav Rosenlof, Jose Coriano

Triangle Pacific Corporation
Office Building
Dallas, Texas

Jacob Alspector, Glen Fries, Karen Jacobson, Bruce Nagel,
Gustav Rosenlof

deMenil Residence
Houston, Texas

Bruce Nagel, Michael Monsky, Victoria Hage, Daniel Rowen

deMenil Residence
East Hampton, New York

Bruce Nagel, Paul Aferiat, Henry Ayon, Frank Lupo,
Barry McCormick, John Meder, Thomas Phifer, Daniel Rowen,
David Steinman

Block Residence (project)
Wilmington, North Carolina

Bruce Nagel, Daniel Rowen

Einstein Moomjy
Showroom
New York, New York

Joel Bargmann, Jose Coriano, David King

Greenwich Savings Bank
New York, New York

Joel Bargmann, Paul Aferiat, Jose Coriano, Glen Fries,
David King

Reliance Group Holdings, Inc.
Offices
New York, New York

Joel Bargmann, David Knowlton, Joseph Ruocco, Paul Aferiat,
Richard Clarke, Jose Coriano, Jeffrey Feingold, Frank Lupo,
Gustav Rosenlof, David Steinman

Morton L. Janklow & Associates
Offices
New York, New York

Richard Gould, Joseph Ruocco

Lincoln Center for the Performing Arts
Concourse
New York, New York

Gustav Rosenlof, David King, Jacob Alspector

Viereck Residence
Amagansett, New York

Bruce Nagel, Paul Aferiat, Daniel Rowen

Ally & Gargano, Inc.
Offices
New York, New York

Gustav Rosenlof, William Garbus, Robert Anderson,
Richard Gould, Victoria Hage, Barry McCormick,
Fuensanta Nieto

Knoll Furniture
Desk and Credenza System

Gustav Rosenlof, John Petrarca

1980

First City Bank
Bank and Office Building
Houston, Texas

Joel Bargmann, Joseph Ruocco, Robert Anderson,
Victoria Hage, Mark Simon
Urban Architecture, Inc. (Associate Architect)

1981

The Evans Partnership
Office Building
Montvale, New Jersey

Richard Gould
Rotwein & Blake Associated Architects, P.A.
(Associate Architect)

Wick Alumni Center
University of Nebraska
Lincoln, Nebraska

Bruce Nagel, Paul Aferiat, Richard Clarke, David Fukui,
Frank Lupo, Barry McCormick, Jo Merriman, Furensanta Nieto,
Thomas Phifer, David Steinman, Thomas Whitrock

Summit Hotel (project)
New York, New York

Thomas Phifer, Howard Goldstein, Daniel Rowen,
Joseph Ruocco, Earl Swisher, Thomas Whitrock

Arango Apartment
New York, New York

Jose Coriano, Frank Lupo

Westport Public Library
Westport, Connecticut

Bruce Nagel, Dirk Kramer, Bruce Donnally,
Margaret Fitzpatrick, Steven Forman, Johannes Kastner,
Reynold Logan, Reed Morrison, John Petrarca, Daniel Rowen,
Irene Torroella

deMenil Residence
Santa Monica, California

Bruce Nagel, John Meder, Karen Renick

Speculative Office Building (project)
New York, New York

Joel Bargmann, Richard Clarke

deMenil Residence (project)
New York, New York

Bruce Nagel, John Meder, John Petrarca

1982

Gwathmey Siegel & Associates Architects
Offices
New York, New York

William Garbus, Dean Marchetto

Steinberg Apartment
New York, New York

Bruce Nagel, John Petrarca, John Meder

Liberty National Bank (project)
Bank and Office Building
Hobbs, New Mexico

Jacob Alspector, Daniel Rowen

Educational/Arts
Buildings and Projects
see pages 16–37

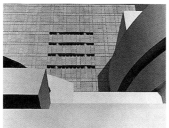

Guggenheim Museum
Addition, Renovation, and Restoration
New York, New York

Jacob Alspector, Pierre Cantacuzene, Gregory Karn, Earl Swisher,
Paul Aferiat, Patricia Cheung, Nancy Clayton, Marc DuBois,
Steven Forman, David Fratianne, Gerald Gendreau, Siamak Hariri,
Anthony Iovino, Dirk Kramer, Daniel Madlansacay, David Mateer,
Jeffrey Murphy, Joseph Ruocco, Gary Shoemaker, Irene Torroella,
Alexandra Villegas, Peter Wiederspahn, Ross Wimer, Stephen Yablon

Nassau Park
Office Building
West Windsor, New Jersey

Jacob Alspector, Dirk Kramer, Margaret Fitzpatrick,
Elizabeth Post, Barry Silberstang, Earl Swisher, Ivan Zaknic

IBM Product Center
Prototype

Jacob Alspector, Steven Forman, Dirk Kramer, Irene Torroella

IBM Product Center
Albany, New York

Jacob Alspector, Steven Forman, Margaret Fitzpatrick

The Evans Partnership
Office Building
Rutherford, New Jersey

Joel Bargmann, Joseph Ruocco, Bruce Donnally,
Christopher Egan, Howard Goldstein, Peter Guggenheimer

The Evans Partnership
Office Building
Paramus, New Jersey

Joel Bargmann, Thomas Phifer, Earl Swisher, Christopher Egan,
Joseph Ruocco

The Evans Partnership
Office Building
Parsippany, New Jersey

Thomas Phifer, Timothy Greer, Peter Guggenheimer,
Dirk Kramer, Reed Morrison, Daniel Rowen, Irene Torroella

Beverly Hills Civic Center
Competition (project)
Beverly Hills, California

Jacob Alspector, Thomas Phifer, Daniel Rowen,
Gustav Rosenlof, Margaret Fitzpatrick, Steven Forman,
Frank Lupo, Dirk Kramer, Alexandra Villegas,
Howard Goldstein, Earl Swisher, Irene Torroella,
David Steinman

deMenil Table Series
ICF

Millan Galland

Tapestry
V'Soske

1983

Residential
Buildings and Projects
see pages 224–227

Spielberg Apartment
New York, New York

Jose Coriano, Reese Owens

Corporate
Buildings and Projects
see pages 122–127

International Design Center I & II
Showroom Buildings
Long Island City, New York

Bruce Nagel, Bruce Donnally
Stephen Lepp, P.C., Architects & Planners (Associate Architect)

The Evans Partnership (project)
Office Building
Piscataway, New Jersey

Thomas Phifer, Daniel Rowen, Dirk Kramer

Educational/Arts
Buildings and Projects
see pages 38–45

American Museum of the Moving Image
Astoria, New York

Jacob Alspector, Paul Aferiat, Timothy Greer, Jude LeBlanc,
Jay Measley, Alissa Bucher, Pierre Cantacuzene,
Stephen Connors, Steven Forman, Lee Hagen, Dirk Kramer,
Ming Leung, Shalini Taneja

New York Public Library
Yorkville Branch
New York, New York

Gustav Rosenlof, Johannes Kastner, Joan Jasper

Residential
Buildings and Projects
see pages 228–235

Garey Residence
Kent, Connecticut

Jose Coriano, Frank Lupo

Swid Apartment II
New York, New York

Jose Coriano

Bower and Gardner II
Law Offices
New York, New York

Gustav Rosenlof, Jay Measley, Millan Galland

1984

Educational/Arts
Buildings and Projects
see pages 46–53

The John Berry Sports Center
Dartmouth College
Hanover, New Hampshire

Jacob Alspector, Joseph Ruocco, William Gilliland,
Siamak Hariri, Johannes Kastner, Reese Owens,
Peter Wiederspahn, Neil Troiano

Educational/Arts
Buildings and Projects
see pages 56–63

School of Agriculture
Administration/Academic Building
Cornell University
Ithaca, New York

Thomas Levering, Ronald Ellis, Daniel Rowen, Paul Cha,
Thomas Demetrion, Peter Guggenheimer, Joan Jasper,
Thomas Lekometros, Jay Levy, Wolfram Wohr

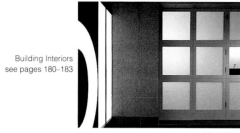

Building Interiors
see pages 180–183

Knoll International Showroom
Chicago, Illinois

Jacob Alspector, Paul Aferiat, Barry McCormick,
Richard Velsor, John Petrarca

Sagner Residence (project)
Essex Fells, New Jersey

Thomas Phifer, Steven Forman, Johannes Kastner,
Richard Velsor

Ogilvy & Mather Offices
Chicago, Illinois

Gustav Rosenlof, Richard Velsor, Joan Jasper, Reynold Logan,
Jay Measley

Tuxedo Dinnerware
Swid Powell Design

1985

Educational/Arts
Buildings and Projects
see pages 64–71

Fieldhouse and Basketball Arena
Cornell University
Ithaca, New York

Peter Guggenheimer, Ronald Ellis, E. Jon Frishmen,
Ming Leung, Jay Levy, Jeffrey Murphy, Guy Oliver,
Joan Pierpoline, Thomas Savory, Joseph Tanney,
Gary Shoemaker, Richard Velsor

Corporate
Buildings and Projects
see pages 134–137

IBM Corporation
Office Building and Distribution Center
Greensboro, North Carolina

Thomas Phifer, Richard Velsor, Philip Dordai, Malka Friedman,
Diane Grey, Thomas Lekometros

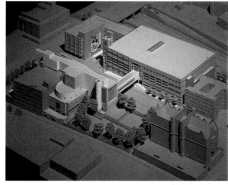

Academic and Multipurpose Building
Eugenio Maria de Hostos Community College
The City University of New York
Bronx, New York

Jacob Alspector, Thomas Lekometros, Stephen Yablon,
Jeffrey Bacon, Rustico Bernardo, Karen Brenner,
Pierre Cantacuzene, Nancy Clayton, Thomas Demetrion,
Marc DuBois, Ronald Ellis, Steven Forman, Peter Franck,
Gerald Gendreau, Anthony Iovino, Johannes Kastner,
Rayme Kuniyuki, Ming Leung, Dean Maltz, Paul Mitchell,
Peter Pawlak, Joseph Ruocco, Bryce Sanders, Thomas Savory,
George Selkirk, Lilla Smith, Earl Swisher, Joseph Tanney,
Dickens van der Werff, Richard Velsor, Peter Wiederspahn,
Ross Wimer

Corporate
Buildings and Projects
see pages 128–133

Solomon Equities, Inc.
Office Building
New York, New York

Bruce Donnally, Gerald Gendreau, Keith Goich,
Sanford Berger, Marc DuBois, Dean Maltz, Li Wen
Emery Roth and Sons (Associate Architect)

Educational/Arts
Buildings and Projects
see pages 82–87

Theater Arts and Fine Arts Building
State University of New York at Buffalo
Amherst, New York

Dirk Kramer, Philip Dordai, Thomas Levering, Jeffrey Bacon,
Nancy Clayton, Rayme Kuniyuki, Lee Ledbetter, Lilla Smith,
Earl Swisher
Scanfidi & Moore (Associate Architect)

Financial Benefits Research Group
Offices
Roseland, New Jersey

Tsun-Kin Tam, Paul Boardman, Thomas Lekometros,
Ming Leung

Residential
Buildings and Projects
see pages 236–243

Spielberg Residence
East Hampton, New York

Jose Coriano, Kerry Moran

Opel Residence
Shelburne, Vermont

Paul Aferiat, Reynold Logan

Lexecon, Inc.
Offices
Chicago, Illinois

Thomas Levering, Barry McCormick, Pierre Cantacuzene, Thomas Demetrion, Ronald Ellis, Steven Hennebery, Joan Jasper

1986

Maguire Thomas Partnership
Leasing Offices
Dallas, Texas

Philip Dordai, Thomas Lekometros

Steinberg Residence
East Hampton, New York

Gustav Rosenlof, Joan Jasper, Malka van Bemmelen, Joan Pierpoline

College of Architecture Building
University of North Carolina
Charlotte, North Carolina

Bruce Donnally, Dirk Kramer, Jay Measley, Peter Wiederspahn
The FWA Group (Associate Architect)

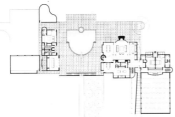

Gimelstob Residence
New Vernon, New Jersey

Peter Guggenheimer, Jay Levy, Gregory Epstein

Building Interiors
see pages 188–195

Herman Miller
Showroom
Long Island City, New York

Paul Aferiat, Ming Leung, Gerald Gendreau

Birdhouse
The Parrish Art Museum
Southampton, New York

Educational/Arts
Buildings and Projects
see pages 94–101

North Campus Dining Building
Oberlin College
Oberlin, Ohio

Bruce Donnally, Samuel Anderson, Rustico Bernardo,
Deborah Cohen, Jay Levy, Jeffrey Murphy, Peter Wiederspahn,
Stephen Yablon

Building Interiors
see pages 196–199

1987

The Georgetown Group, Inc.
Offices
New York, New York

Jose Coriano, Tsun-Kin Tam, Thomas Lekometros,
Gustav Rosenlof

Bower and Gardner III
Law Offices
New York, New York

Joseph Ruocco, Jeffrey Bacon, Philip Dordai, Lilla Smith

McCann-Erickson Worldwide
Offices
New York, New York

Richard Velsor, Thomas Levering, Keith Goich, Anthony Iovino,
Dean Maltz, Joseph Tanney

Building Interiors
see pages 206–211

Building Interiors
see pages 200–205

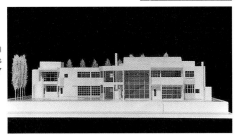

Residential
Buildings and Projects
see pages 268–277

Educational/Arts
Buildings and Projects
see pages 72–77

Educational/Arts
Buildings and Projects
see pages 106–119

D'Arcy Masius Benton & Bowles, Inc.
Offices
New York, New York

Gustav Rosenlof, Donald Tapert, Paul Aferiat, Deborah Cohen,
Gerald Gendreau, Gregory Karn, Dirk Kramer, Jeffrey Murphy,
Bryce Sanders, Gary Shoemaker

SBK Entertainment World, Inc.
Offices
New York, New York

Tsun-Kin Tam, Gregory Karn, Jeffrey Bacon, Paul Boardman,
Philip Dordai, Marc DuBois, Dirk Kramer, Thomas Lekometros,
Jay Levy, Lilla Smith, Malka van Bemmelen

1988   Oceanfront Residence
California

Gerald Gendreau, Anthony Iovino, Nancy Clayton,
Gregory Epstein, Paul Mitchell

College of Engineering
Theory Center Building
Cornell University
Ithaca, New York

Thomas Levering, Paul Boardman, David Biagi, Ronald Ellis,
Gerald Gendreau, Dirk Kramer, Joseph Tanney,
Malka van Bemmelen

Werner Otto Hall
Busch Reisinger Museum/Fine Arts Library
The Fogg Museum
Harvard University
Cambridge, Massachusetts

Bruce Donnally, Samuel Anderson, Johannes Kastner,
Rustico Bernardo, Joan Jasper, Paul Mitchell

McDonough Art Museum
Youngstown State University
Youngstown, Ohio

Thomas Levering, David Biagi

Smith Kline & French (project)
Corporate Headquarters
Upper Merion Township, Pennsylvania

Gerald Gendreau, Earl Swisher, Deborah Cohen,
Emanuel Garcia, Bryce Sanders

Rosen Townhouses
New York, New York

Peter Guggenheimer, Joseph Tanney, Paul Mitchell

Residential
Buildings and Projects
see pages 264–267

Gwathmey Apartment
New York, New York

Tsun-Kin Tam, Paul Aferiat, Joseph Ruocco

Educational/Arts
Buildings and Projects
see pages 102–105

Center for Jewish Life
Duke University
Durham, North Carolina

Thomas Levering, David Biagi, Patricia Bosch-Melendez,
Deborah Cohen, Mark Rylander, Malka van Bemmelen,
Dickens van der Werff

Due Restaurant
New York, New York

Jose Coriano

Chicago Dinnerware
Swid Powell Design

Courtney Vase and Candlestick
Swid Powell Design

1989

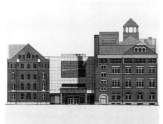

School of Architecture (project)
Pratt Institute
  Brooklyn, New York

Bruce Donnally, Nancy Clayton, Ross Wimer

Leavitt Advertising/Hanover House
Offices
  Weehawken, New Jersey

Gerald Gendreau, David Hendershot,
Rayme Kuniyuki, Joseph Tanney

Winfrey Apartment (project)
  Chicago, Illinois

Thomas Lekometros, Karen Brenner, Stephen Yablon

Corporate
Buildings and Projects
see pages 152–155

The David Geffen Company
Office Building
  Beverly Hills, California

Dirk Kramer, Lilla Smith, Juan Miro, Joseph Ruocco

Geffen/Salick
Office Building
  Beverly Hills, California

Dirk Kramer, Rayme Kuniyuki, Edward Arcari, Juan Miro,
Lilla Smith

Corporate
Buildings and Projects
see pages 138–147

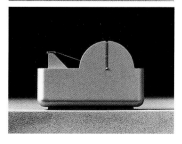

Contemporary Resort Convention Center
Walt Disney World
Lake Buena Vista, Florida

Joseph Ruocco, Rayme Kuniyuki, Keith Howie, Edward Arcari,
David Hendershot, Michelle Kolb

Koppelman Apartment
New York, New York

Dirk Kramer, Lilla Smith, Jorge Castillo, Anthony Iovino

Gymnasium
State University at Oneonta
Oneonta, New York

Joseph Ruocco, Edward Arcari, Keith Howie, Loretta Leung,
Frank Thaler, Karen Renick

Spielberg Guest House
East Hampton, New York

Jose Coriano, Daniel Sullivan

Knoll Furniture
Derby Desk

Gustav Rosenlof, David Biagi

Knoll Accessories (project)

Gustav Rosenlof, David Biagi

Petrafina Candlestick (project)

David Biagi, Elizabeth Skowronek

Courtney Bowl
Swid Powell Design

1990   BioTech Laboratory Building
State University of New York at Syracuse
Syracuse, New York

Thomas Levering, Mark Rylander, Patricia Bosch-Melendez,
Sean Flynn, Peter Brooks

Staller Residence
Old Field, New York

Gustav Rosenlof, Richard Lanier, Deborah Cohen,
Thomas Lekometros, Stephen Yablon

Meyer Residence
Malibu, California

Dirk Kramer, Lilla Smith, Meta Brunzema, Juan Miro,
Daniel Sullivan

Corporate
Buildings and Projects
see pages 148–151

Bonnet Creek Golf Clubhouse
Walt Disney World
Lake Buena Vista, Florida

Joseph Ruocco, Edward Arcari, Richard Lanier,
Peter Guggenheimer, Loretta Leung

327

Corporate
Buildings and Projects
see pages 170–177

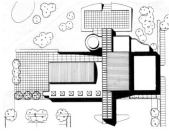

Golf Clubhouse
Euro–Disney
Marne-la-Vallée, France

Gerald Gendreau, Mark Rylander, Gregory Epstein,
Anthony Iovino
Rey Grange & Jelensperger (Associate Architect)

Residential
Buildings and Projects
see pages 278–283

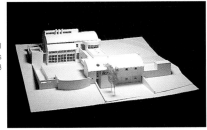

Bechtler Residence
Zumikon, Switzerland

Bruce Donnally, Nancy Clayton, Thomas Lewis, Sylvia Becker
Pfister & Schiess Architekten (Associate Architect)

Residential
Buildings and Projects
see pages 284–291

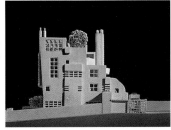

Chen Residence
Taipei, Taiwan

Jacob Alspector, Gregory Karn, Gregory Epstein, Tsun-Kin Tam

Building Interiors
see pages 212–215

Ronald S. Lauder
Offices
New York, New York

Tsun-Kin Tam, Lilla Smith

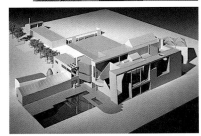

Gagosian Residence
East Hampton, New York

Gustav Rosenlof

Anniversary Dinnerware
Swid Powell Design

American Airlines Dinnerware
Swid Powell Design

Building Interiors
see pages 216–221

1991   The Capital Group, Inc.
Offices
West Los Angeles, California

Dirk Kramer, Karen Renick, Peter Brooks, Meta Brunzema,
Kathleen Byrne, Jay Levy, Lilla Smith, Christopher Coe

PepsiCo Corporate Center
Dining Facilities
Purchase, New York

Thomas Levering, Patricia Bosch-Melendez, Sean Flynn,
David Biagi

Sony Entertainment, Inc.
Corporate Headquarters
New York, New York

Richard Velsor, Bruce Donnally, Gustav Rosenlof,
Stephen Yablon, Peter Brooks, Kathleen Byrne, Steven Forman,
Michael Girimonti, Pascal Jeambon, Barbara Krause,
Richard Lanier, David Mateer, Tsun-Kin Tam, Frank Thaler

Social Sciences Building
University of California at San Diego
La Jolla, California

Bruce Donnally, Nancy Clayton, Richard Lanier, Thomas Lewis
Brown Gimber Rodriguez Park (Associate Architect)

Science, Industry, and Business Library
The New York Public Library
New York, New York

Thomas Levering, Jacob Alspector, Daniel Sullivan,
Earl Swisher

Disney Golf Course
Prototype Residence
Euro–Disney
Marne-la-Vallée, France

Gerald Gendreau, Harry Elson, Gregory Epstein,
Anthony Iovino

Corporate
Buildings and Projects
see pages 156–165

Stadtportalhäuser
Competition (project)
Frankfurt am Main, Germany

Jacob Alspector, Gregory Karn, Edward Arcari,
Theodora Betow, Peter Brooks, Meta Brunzema,
Pierre Cantacuzene, Bruce Donnally, Barbara Krause,
Richard Lanier, David Mateer, Peter Pawlak,
Elizabeth Skowronek, Frank Thaler

Master Plan, Broad Building, Academic I,
Student Activities Center
Pitzer College
Claremont, California

Gerald Gendreau, Thomas Lewis, Gregory Epstein,
Christine Straw

1992

Convention Center and Hotel
Euro–Disney
Marne-la-Vallée, France

Joseph Ruocco, Gregory Epstein, Richard Lucas, Juan Miro,
Daniel Sullivan

Corporate
Buildings and Projects
see pages 166–169

The Henry Art Gallery
Addition and Renovation
University of Washington
Seattle, Washington

Bruce Donnally, Nancy Clayton, Richard Lucas
Loschky, Marquardt & Nesholm (Associate Architect)

Residential
Buildings and Projects
see pages 292–297

Villa Austin
Austin, Texas

Gustav Rosenlof, Juan Miro, Meta Brunzema, Sean Flynn

March–April 1986   Modern Redux: Critical Alternatives for Architecture in the Next Decade
New York University, Grey Art Gallery and Study Center
New York, New York

May–July 1987   Architects Design Birdhouses
The Parrish Art Museum
Southampton, New York

April 1988   ADPSR Benefit Exhibition and Auction
Max Protetch Gallery
New York, New York

June–August 1989   New York Architektur, 1970–1990
Deutches Architektur Museum
Frankfurt, Germany

April 1990   Charles Gwathmey and Robert Siegel: Projects and Furniture for Knoll
Knoll International
Tokyo, Japan

May–June 1991   Charles Gwathmey and Robert Siegel Architects, New York: Recent Works
Architektur Forum Zurich
Zurich, Switzerland

September 23–October 11 1991   The Guggenheim Museum, New York City: The Addition, Renovation,
Expansion, and Restoration by Gwathmey Siegel & Associates Architects
Harvard University Graduate School of Design
Cambridge, Massachusetts

January–March 1992   Architects for Snoopy
Montreal Museum of Fine Arts
Montreal, Quebec

November 1992   Five Architects—Twenty Years Later
University of Maryland School of Architecture
College Park, Maryland

Exhibits

1982

The American Institute of Architects
Firm Award

Progressive Architecture
Design Award
  deMenil Residence
  East Hampton, New York

Progressive Architecture
Design Award
  University of Nebraska
  Wick Alumni Center
  Lincoln, Nebraska

Architectural Record
Record Interior
  Morton L. Janklow & Associates Offices
  New York, New York

Architectural Record
Record House
  Viereck Residence
  Amagansett, New York

AIA New York Chapter
Distinguished Architecture Award
  Viereck Residence
  Amagansett, New York

Institute of Business Designers
Product Design Award
  Knoll Desks and Credenzas

AIA Los Angeles Chapter
Design Award
  deMenil Residence
  Santa Monica, California

1983

AIA New York Chapter
Medal of Honor

Interiors
Design Award
  Gwathmey Siegel & Associates Offices
  New York, New York

1984

AIA National Honor Award
  Taft Residence
  Cincinnati, Ohio

Architectural Record
Record Interior
  Arango Apartment
  New York, New York

AIA New York Chapter
Distinguished Architecture Award
  First City Bank Building
  Houston, Texas

New York State Association of Architects
Design Award
  deMenil Residence
  East Hampton, New York

New York State Association of Architects
Design Award
  Westover School
  Library and Science Building
  Middlebury, Connecticut

1985

The American Society of Landscape Architects
Honor Award
  deMenil Residence
  East Hampton, New York

Architectural Record
Record Interior
  Spielberg Apartment
  New York, New York

AIA New York Chapter
Distinguished Architecture Award
  deMenil Residence
  East Hampton, New York

AIA New York Chapter
Distinguished Architecture Award
  Arango Apartment
  New York, New York

1986

AIA New York Chapter
Unbuilt Project Award
  Cornell University
  School of Agriculture
  Administrative/Academic Building
  Ithaca, New York

Municipal Art Society of New York
Certificate of Merit
  International Design Center
  Long Island City, New York

AIA Connecticut Chapter
Distinguished Architecture Award
  Westover School
  Library and Science Building
  Middlebury, Connecticut

1987

AIA New York Chapter
Distinguished Architecture Award
  Westover School
  Library and Science Building
  Middlebury, Connecticut

The American Library Association
Award of Excellence
  Westover School
  Library and Science Building
  Middlebury, Connecticut

The New York State Association of Architects
Design Award
  International Design Center
  Long Island City, New York

Interiors
Design Award
  International Design Center
  Long Island City, New York

1988

Architectural Record
Record House
  Garey Residence
  Kent, Connecticut

Architectural Record
Record House
  Spielberg Residence
  East Hampton, New York

Architectural Record
Record House
  Opel Residence
  Shelburne, Vermont

The Art Commission of the City of New York
Excellence in Design Award
  Eugenio Maria de Hostos Community College
  Academic and Multipurpose Building
  The City University of New York
  Bronx, New York

The City Club of New York
Bard Award
  International Design Center
  Queens, New York

AIA National Honor Award
  Westover School
  Library and Science Building
  Middlebury, Connecticut

1990

AIA North Carolina Chapter
Honor Award
  University of North Carolina
  College of Architecture Building
  Charlotte, North Carolina

New York State Association of Architects
Lifetime Achievement Award

1991

AIA New York Chapter
Distinguished Architecture Award
  School of Agriculture Building
  Cornell University
  Ithaca, New York

1992

AIA New York Chapter
Distinguished Architecture Award
  Contemporary Resort Convention Center
  Walt Disney World
  Lake Buena Vista, Florida

AIA New York Chapter
Distinguished Architecture Award
  Opel Residence
  Shelburne, Vermont

Awards

Charles Gwathmey

Charles Gwathmey attended the University of Pennsylvania School of Architecture from 1956 to 1959 and received his master of architecture degree from Yale University in 1962, where he was awarded the William Wirt Winchester Fellowship as well as a Fulbright Grant to study in France. In 1970, Gwathmey became the youngest architect to receive the Brunner Prize from the American Academy Institute of Arts and Letters and in 1974 was the only architect named in the "Leadership in America" issue of *Time* magazine.

In 1981 he was elected a Fellow of the American Institute of Architects. In 1988 he was the recipient of the first Yale School of Architecture Alumni Award in the Arts, and in 1989 he received the Guild Hall Lifetime Achievement Award in the Arts.

Charles Gwathmey has maintained a strong interest in pedagogical issues. He was president of the board of trustees of the Institute of Architecture and Urban Studies in 1979. In 1983 he was the Davenport Professor and, in 1991, Bishop Professor at Yale University. In 1985 he was the Eliot Noyes Visiting Professor at Harvard University. Gwathmey has maintained faculty positions at Pratt Institute, The Cooper Union, Princeton University, Columbia University, the University of Texas, and the University of California at Los Angeles.

Robert Siegel

Robert Siegel received his bachelor of architecture degree from Pratt Institute in 1962 and his master of architecture degree from Harvard University in 1963. In 1981 he served as vice president of the American Institute of Architects New York Chapter, and from 1982 to 1988 he served as chairman on the Pratt Institute Board of Visitors, an advisory group to the School of Architecture. Siegel was awarded the Pratt Institute Centennial Alumni Award in Architecture in 1988 and was elected a Fellow of the American Institute of Architects in 1991. Throughout his professional career he has served as a design critic, juror, and lecturer for architecture schools and professional organizations.

Gwathmey Siegel & Associates Architects

In 1982 Gwathmey Siegel & Associates Architects became the youngest firm ever to be awarded the American Institute of Architects' highest honor—the Firm Award—for "approaching every project with a fresh eye, a meticulous attention to detail, a keen appreciation for environmental and economic concerns, an unswerving dedication to design excellence, and a strong belief in collaborative effort. This firm and its principals are living examples of the highest standards of the profession."

Both Charles Gwathmey and Robert Siegel received the Medal of Honor from the American Institute of Architects New York Chapter in 1983 "for their distinction in evolving one of the most creative practices in our time and for the influence of their practice on architects and students of architecture."

They were inducted into the *Interior Design Magazine* Hall of Fame in 1988 and in 1990 were the recipients of the Lifetime Achievement Award from the New York State Society of Architects.

Biographies

Charles Gwathmey and Robert Siegel

Associates

Paul Aferiat
Jacob Alspector
Jose Coriano
Bruce Donnally
Gerald Gendreau
Dirk Kramer
Peter Guggenheimer
Thomas Levering
Bruce Nagel
Thomas Phifer
Gustav Rosenlof
Joseph Ruocco
Tsun-Kin Tam
Richard Velsor

Architects

Samuel Anderson
Robin Andrade
Edward Arcari
Jeffrey Bacon
John Belbusti
Sanford Berger
Rustico Bernardo
David Biagi
Paul Boardman
Patricia Bosch-Melendez
Karen Brenner
Peter Brooks
Patricia Brukman
Meta Brunzema
Alissa Bucher
Kathleen Byrne
Pierre Cantacuzene
Jorge Castillo
Alberto Catania
Paul Cha
Patricia Cheung
Noel Clark
Nancy Clayton
Christopher Coe
Deborah Cohen
Stephen Connors
Benjamin Curatolo
Thomas Demetrion
Philip Dordai
Marc DuBois
Christopher Egan
Ronald Ellis
Harry Elson
Gregory Epstein
Margaret Fitzpatrick

Sean Flynn
Steven Forman
Peter Franck
David Fratianne
Malka Friedman
E. Jon Frishman
Millan Galland
Emanuel Garcia
William Gilliland
Michael Girimonti
Keith Goich
Timothy Greer
Diane Grey
David Hacin
Victoria Hage
Lee Hagen
Ted E. Halsey
Siamak Hariri
David Hendershot
Steven Hennebery
Keith Howie
Craig Hunt
Anthony Iovino
Joan Jasper
Pascal Jeambon
James Jorgensen
James Kalvelage
Gregory Karn
Johannes Kastner
Matthew Keeler
Lucille Kelly
David Knowlton
Michelle Kolb
Barbara Krause
Rayme Kuniyuki
Richard Lanier
Jude LeBlanc
Lee Ledbetter
Thomas Lekometros
Ming Leung
Jay Levy
Thomas Lewis
Reynold Logan
Robert Luntz
Frank Lupo
Daniel Madlansacay
Dean Maltz
David Mateer
Barry McCormick
Jay Measley
Juan Miro
Paul Mitchell
Kerry Moran
Reed Morrison
Jeffrey Murphy

Andrew Neuberger
Guy Oliver
Reese Owens
Peter Pawlak
Malcolm Payne
John Petrarca
Joan Pierpoline
Michael Regan
Luke Regier
Karen Renick
Miguel Rivera
Gary Rosenthal
Daniel Rowen
Mark Rylander
Bryce Sanders
Thomas Savory
George Selkirk
Gary Shoemaker
Elizabeth Skowronek
Lilla Smith
Daniel Sullivan
Earl Swisher
Shalini Taneja
Joseph Tanney
Donald Tapert
Frank Thaler
Irene Torroella
Neil Troiano
Malka van Bemmelen
Dickens van der Werff
Peter Wiederspahn
Scott Williams
Ross Wimer
Wolfram Wohr
Stephen Yablon

Interns

Reja Bakhshandegi
Sylvia Becker
Theodora Betow
Richard Blender
Renee Bolmeijer
Philippe Bonhote
Tracy Brown
David Buckman
Keith Carlson
Ike Cheung
Robert Choeff
Jiwon Choi
Vincent Cortina
Silvia Dainese
Stephane Defossez
Peter Di Salvo

Joseph Eisner
Klause Elz
Viviana Frank
Shepherd Frankel
Francesco Fresa
Olivier Galetti
David Gissen
Kate Glass
Mario Gooden
Paul Grabowski
Beatriz Guijarro
David Hacin
Laurie Haefele
Joseph Hsu
Celina Hung
Radu Iliou
Carole Iselin
Jon Kastl
Darragh Kelvie
Shirin Kermanschachi
Ada Kny
Beth Kostman
Elizabeth Kraft
Douglas Kupfer
Frank Kutschera
Thomas Kwong
Andres Lopez
Richard Lucas
Peter Lusk
Loretta Leung
Dean Maltz
Peter Mariani
Jeffrey Matz
Angela Mensing
Miguel Mesas
Claude Meyers
Christopher Middleton
Curtis Miller
Juan Miro
Anthony Moran
Steven O'Reilly
Irene Parrandier
Jason Pearson
Albert Pece
Astrid Perlbinder
James Pertusi
Michelle Pfeiffer
Laurie Porcari
Brad Prescott
Becky Pugh
Jurgen Raab
Carlene Ramus
Brian Reiff
Morgan Rolontz
Joseph Rosa

Charles Russell
Kevin Saumell
Heinrich Sauter
Amar Sen
Claire Sevaux
Stefan Spitzer
Christine Straw
Charles Szoradi
Shalini Taneja
Ivo Vanhamme
Robert Villard
Rainer Walder
Susan Watt
Li Wen
Scott Williams
Nina Wolff
Tricia Yulkowski
Ann Zollinger

Administration

Alex Calderone
Adrienne Catropa
Susan Channell
Jeffrey Cohen
Patricia Grana
Una Heron
Michael Janiak
Jennifer Lewis
Beth Littman
Jacque McKinzie
Carla Murray
Robin Noble
Judy Oramas
Jennifer Pirwitz
Amber Poole
Daphne Poser
Reginald Proctor
Jose St. Marthe
Susan Scott
Vikki Stark
Charles Tabick
Shelley Valentino
Edwin Van Gorder
Sandra Volts

Office Staff

Jamie Ardiles-Arce

    Buildings, Projects, Furniture, and Objects:
    1979   Reliance Group Holdings
    1982   Gwathmey Siegel & Associates Architects Offices

Farshid Assassi/Assassi Productions

    Oceanfront Residence
    All photographs

Otto Baitz

    Buildings, Projects, Furniture, and Objects:
    1976   Thomas & Betts Corporation
    1976   Benenson Residence
    1977   Lincoln Center for the Performing Arts
    1977   FDM Productions
    1977   The Evans Partnership, Parsippany
    1977   The Evans Partnership, New York
    1981   The Evans Partnership, Montvale
    1982   Nassau Park
    1982   The Evans Partnership, Rutherford
    1982   The Evans Partnership, Parsippany

Luc Boegly/Archipress

    Golf Clubhouse
    Euro-Disney
    All photographs

Tom Bonner

    The Capital Group
    All photographs

Steven Brooke

    Steinberg Residence
    All photographs

Richard Bryant/Arcaid

    John Berry Sports Center
    Dartmouth College
    All photographs
    International Design Center I & II
    Photographs on pp. 122, 126, and 127
    IBM Greensboro
    All photographs
    except p. 135 bottom right
    Herman Miller Showroom
    All photographs
    Spielberg Apartment
    All photographs
    Garey Residence
    All photographs
    Spielberg Residence
    All photographs
    except p. 236 left
    Opel Residence
    All photographs

    Buildings, Projects, Furniture, and Objects:
    1982   Steinberg Apartment

Orlando R. Cabanban

    Buildings, Projects, Furniture, and Objects:
    1974   Vidal Sassoon Salon, Chicago

Louis Checkman

    IBM Greensboro
    Page 135 bottom right
    Theater Arts and Fine Arts Building
    State University of New York at Buffalo
    Page 83

    Buildings, Projects, Furniture, and Objects:
    1970   Eskilson Residence
    1971   Elia-Bash Residence
    1973   Geffen Residence
    1977   Northgate Housing
    1982   Beverly Hills Civic Center
    1986   Birdhouse

George Cserna

    Buildings, Projects, Furniture, and Objects:
    1979   Morton L. Janklow & Associates

David Franzen

    Buildings, Projects, Furniture, and Objects:
    1969   Dormitory, Dining, and Student Union Building
          State University of New York at Purchase

Jeff Goldberg/Esto

    Guggenheim Museum Addition
    Photographs on pp. 17, 20–29, 30 top, and 32–36
    American Museum of the Moving Image
    All photographs
    except p. 38 bottom
    School of Agriculture
    Cornell University
    Photographs on pp. 56–59 and 62
    Fieldhouse and Basketball Arena
    Cornell University
    Photographs on pp. 66 top and 69–71
    Academic and Multipurpose Building
    Eugenio Maria de Hostos Community College
    The City University of New York
    Photographs on pp. 78–79
    Theater Arts and Fine Arts Building
    State University of New York at Buffalo
    Page 82
    Solomon Equities, Inc.
    All photographs
    Contemporary Resort Convention Center
    Walt Disney World
    All photographs

    Buildings, Projects, Furniture, and Objects:
    1989   Leavitt Advertising/Hanover House

Photography Credits

all other photography courtesy of Gwathmey Siegel & Associates Architects

David Hirsch

    Buildings, Projects, Furniture, and Objects:
      1964   Miller Residence

Wolfgang Hoyt

    Academic and Multipurpose Building
    Eugenio Maria de Hostos Community College
    The City University of New York
    Photographs on pp. 80–81

Timothy Hursley

    School of Agriculture
    Cornell University
    Photographs on pp. 55, 60, 61, and 63
    Fieldhouse and Basketball Arena
    Cornell University
    Photographs on pp. 55, 64, 65, 66 bottom, and 68
    Theory Center at the College of Engineering
    Cornell University
    All photographs
    International Design Center I & II
    Photographs on pp. 123–125

    Buildings, Projects, Furniture, and Objects:
      1979   Library and Science Building, Westover School

Barbara Karant

    Knoll International Showroom
    All photographs

Elliot Kaufman

    Bonnet Creek Golf Clubhouse
    Walt Disney World
    All photographs
    SBK Entertainment World, Inc.
    All photographs

Balthazer Korab, Ltd.

    Buildings, Projects, Furniture, and Objects:
      1978   Sycamore Place Elderly Housing
      1978   Pence Street Family Housing

Nathaniel Lieberman

    Center for Jewish Life
    Duke University
    All photographs

    Buildings, Projects, Furniture, and Objects:
      1979   Greenwich Savings Bank
      1982   The Evans Partnership, Paramus
      1988   Smith Kline & French

Mancia/Bodner

    Bechtler Residence
    All photographs

William Maris

    Buildings, Projects, Furniture, and Objects:
      1965   Herlinger-Bristol Ltd.
      1966   Straus Residence
      1967   Sedacca Residence
      1967   Goldberg Residence
      1968   Cooper Residence
      1968   Steel Residences I & II
      1968   Service Building and Heating Plant
      1969   Brooklyn Friends School
      1969   Gwathmey Siegel Architects Offices
      1970   Tolan Residence
      1973   Pearl's Restaurant
      1974   Transammonia Corporation

Norman McGrath

    The Georgetown Group, Inc.
    All photographs

    Buildings, Projects, Furniture, and Objects:
      1965   Gwathmey Residence and Studio
      1970   Whig Hall, Princeton University
      1972   Cohn Residence
      1972   Whitney Road Housing
      1974   Kislevitz Residence
      1974   Vidal Sassoon Salon, New York
      1974   Vidal Sassoon Salon, Beverly Hills
      1974   Vidal Sassoon Corporate Offices
      1975   Student Apartment Housing, SUNY, Purchase
      1975   Bower and Gardner
      1975   The Evans Partnership, Piscataway
      1975   U.S. Steakhouse Restaurant
      1975   Barber Oil Corporation
      1976   Haupt Residence
      1976   Weitz Residence
      1976   Swirl, Inc.
      1976   Swid Apartment I
      1977   Poster Originals, Ltd.
      1977   Garey Shirtmakers
      1977   Geffen Apartment
      1977   Belkin Memorial Room
      1977   AT&T Office Building
      1978   Shezan Restaurant
      1978   Giorgio Armani, Inc.
      1979   deMenil Residence, East Hampton
      1979   Lincoln Center for the Performing Arts Concourse
      1979   Viereck Residence
      1979   Ally & Gargano, Inc.
      1981   Arango Apartment
      1981   Westport Public Library
      1982   IBM Product Center
      1983   International Design Center I & II
      1983   New York Public Library, Yorkville Branch
      1983   Swid Apartment II
      1983   Bower and Gardner II
      1985   Financial Benefits Research Group
      1987   Bower and Gardner III
      1988   Due Restaurant
      1990   Gagosian Residence

Ira Montgomery

    Buildings, Projects, Furniture, and Objects:
      1986   Maguire Thomas Partnership

Gregory Murphy

    Lexecon, Inc.
    All photographs

Richard Payne

Buildings, Projects, Furniture, and Objects:
1975	Damson Oil Corporation
1975	Northpoint Office Building
1976	East Campus Student Housing and Academic Center, Columbia University
1977	Taft Residence
1978	Amax Petroleum Corporation
1979	Triangle Pacific Corporation
1979	deMenil Residence, Houston
1980	First City Bank

Jock Pottle/Esto

The David Geffen Company
All photographs
Stadtportalhäuser
All photographs
Convention Center and Hotel
Euro-Disney
All photographs
Chen Residence
All photographs
Villa Austin
All photographs

Buildings, Projects, Furniture, and Objects:
1989	Geffin/Salick
1989	Gymnasium, State University at Oneonta
1990	Gagosian Residence
1991	Social Sciences Building, UCSD
1991	Disney Golf Course, Prototype Residence
1991	Master Plan, Broad Building, Academic I, Student Activities Center, Pitzer College

David Ramsey

College of Architecture
University of North Carolina
Page 91 top

Marvin Rand

Buildings, Projects, Furniture, and Objects:
1974	Vidal Sassoon Salon, La Costa
1981	de Menil Residence, Santa Monica

George Raustiala

Buildings, Projects, Furniture, and Objects:
1973	Sagner Residence
1973	St. Casmir Housing
1975	Nassau County Art Center
1975	One Times Square
1976	Hyatt Hotel and Casino
1979	Hines Residence

Steve Rosenthal

Buildings, Projects, Furniture, and Objects:
1978	Knoll International Showroom

Sadin Photo Group, Inc.

Buildings, Projects, Furniture, and Objects:
1981	Wick Alumni Center, University of Nebraska
1984	Ogilvy & Mather

Gordon Schenck

College of Architecture
University of North Carlina
All photographs, pp. 88–93
except p. 89 bottom right and p. 91 top

Susan Scott

Buildings, Projects, Furniture, and Objects:
1989	Knoll Accessories

Ezra Stoller/Esto

Buildings, Projects, Furniture, and Objects:
1969	Dunaway Apartment
1971	Cogan Residence

Sarah Strouss

Buildings, Projects, Furniture, and Objects:
1988	McDonough Art Museum

Judith Turner

Guggenheim Museum Addition
Photographs on pp. 16, 18, 19, 30 bottom left and right, 31, and 37

Paul Warchol

North Campus Dining Building
Oberlin College
All photographs
Werner Otto Hall
Harvard University
All photographs
D'Arcy Masius Benton & Bowles, Inc.
All photographs
Offices for Ronald S. Lauder
All photographs
Gwathmey Apartment
All photographs

Buildings, Projects, Furniture, and Objects:
1987	McCann-Erickson Worldwide

Tom Yee

Buildings, Projects, Furniture, and Objects:
1971	New York Apartment
1975	Unger Apartment

courtesy of Knoll International:

Buildings, Projects, Furniture, and Objects:
1979	Knoll Furniture Desk and Credenza
1989	Knoll Furniture Derby Desk

courtesy of Swid Powell:

Buildings, Projects, Furniture, and Objects:
1984	Tuxedo Dinnerware
1988	Chicago Dinnerware
1988	Courtney Vase and Candlestick
1989	Courtney Bowl
1990	Anniversary Dinnerware